Fashion Source Book

Second Edition

KATHRYN McKELVEY

Reader, School of Design
Northumbria University

Blackwell
Publishing

Editorial Offices:
Blackwell Publishing Ltd, 9600 Garsington Road, Oxford OX4 2DQ, UK
  Tel: +44 (0)1865 776868
Blackwell Publishing Professional, 2121 State Avenue, Ames, Iowa 50014-8300, USA
  Tel: +1 515 292 0140
Blackwell Publishing Asia, 550 Swanston Street, Carlton, Victoria 3053, Australia
  Tel: +61 (0)3 8359 1011

First edition published 1996 by Blackwell Science
Second edition published 2006 by Blackwell Publishing
2   2007

ISBN 978-1-4051-2693-9

Library of Congress Cataloging-in-Publication Data
McKelvey, Kathryn.
   Fashion source book/Kathryn McKelvey. – 2nd ed.
   p. cm.
   ISBN 978-1-4051-2693-9 (alk. paper)
   1. Fashion drawing—Pictorial works. I. Title.

TT509.M38 2005
746.9'2–dc22
2005054575

A catalogue record for this title is available from the British Library

Set in Minion by NewGen Imaging Pvt Ltd, Chennai
Printed and bound in India by Replika Press Pvt. Ltd

The publisher's policy is to use permanent paper from mills that operate a sustainable forestry policy, and which has been manufactured from pulp processed using acid-free and elementary chlorine-free practices. Furthermore, the publisher ensures that the text paper and cover board used have met acceptable environmental accreditation standards.

For further information on Blackwell Publishing, visit our website:
www.blackwellpublishing.com

CONTENTS

PREFACE

This second edition of the *Fashion Source Book* hopes to continue to fill a basic need of the fashion student. Novice students take up their respective courses of study with little background in fashion, only an interest in and enthusiasm for the subject. They begin their studies with limited experience in the field of fashion. This has not been much of a problem in the past but, with increased pressure on fashion courses to expand and economise on their teaching programmes, there is a very real concern that basic knowledge may be lacking. This book attempts to redress the balance and provide information that is comprehensive and time saving.

This book offers copyright-free illustrations sourced from costume and fashion (around 70 new designs are added in this edition). The men's, women's and children's figures are devised to give as many realistic/natural variations in pose and body type as possible. They should also give some feeling of how children stand and how they hold things at varying stages of their development. The poses show how, for example, hats sit on children's heads, how different fabrics drape and gather and how print scale may work.

The drawings have been reworked with a more up-to-date technique to show as much relevant fabric representation as possible. The process used was to redraw the line drawings, scan them into Adobe PhotoShop and then, to enrich the line, convert them in Adobe Streamline – they may be saved as vector art (for use in Adobe Illustrator) or, as in this case, raster art for use in PhotoShop. The images were then flooded with patterns and textures (also scanned in and 'defined' as patterns) using the magic wand tool, for selection, and the pattern stamp tool or paint bucket to fill the drawings. Some of the transparency and layering tools were also used.

The flat drawings provide information on how to construct garments, what shapes are possible and how to identify and use the correct terminology when presenting work. Garments included are of historical, ethnic and modern interest. Many new items have been chosen for their interesting 'origins', which can be found in the GLOSSARY. For example the '1940s jumper' on page 141 owes its uneven stripy look to the use of other unravelled jumpers, a necessity of recycling in contribution to the war effort. Other examples are chosen for their 'cut' such as the 1920s coat (page 66) or John Galliano jacket (page 82). Descriptive text of every item is provided in the GLOSSARY to aid in any further specialist research that may be necessary. The type of information provided ranges from the sort of fabrics and colours used, the period from which an article is derived or simply its function in our lives.

In ACCESSORIES a whole page has been attributed to the phenomenon of the 'trainer' (page 164) from specialist sports shoe to fashion shoe with all the interim influences.

The FASHION ILLUSTRATION section shows how to utilise the figures and develop them for fashion purposes.

Each garment or accessory mentioned is placed under a broad heading of what it is. Information is also given as to whether it is menswear, womenswear or childrenswear, more specifically, each clothing item has after its name – menswear, womenswear or girls and boyswear or a mixture, if unisex. There are no sex coding references in ACCESSORIES, PRODUCTION and CONSTRUCTION as these elements can broadly be used to design for either sex.

Each item in the book is seen as a resource. Consequently there are two ways of finding a particular item in the INDEX. The first is as a direct entry under the item's own name; that is, if the name was mentioned in a lecture or presentation and the student was unfamiliar with it, they could refer directly to the index. The second is under the item category, for example, if trousers were being researched then there would be a list of each type of trouser, in alphabetical order, under TROUSERS.

Obviously every single item that has ever been designed is not included, but effort has been made to include items that have a particular name, maybe an interesting cut and have had a function in society.

It must be remembered that this book provides basic information to begin designing. It is the personal development and interpretation of design that makes it new, creative, individual and exciting.

Key points when designing for fashion are:

    Function and market level
    Trend, theme research
    Silhouette, shape
    Colour
    Fabric
    Texture
    Pattern, print
    Detail
    Finish

Design may begin at any of these key points. This book provides information in all of these areas except current trends and colour. The rest is up to you!

Coding description:

™ – trademark

US – American terminology

ACKNOWLEDGEMENTS

I would like to thank colleagues in the School of Design at Northumbria University for advice and support. I would like to thank every author in the Bibliography.

Thanks also to the publishers, Blackwell Publishing, and especially Richard Miles for his support and for giving me another chance to prove myself.

I would also like to thank my husband, Ian, for his never-ending patience in what has been another long but enjoyable project. Thanks also to Emily, Lucy and Jack for their interest and good behaviour while I have been working.

NEWBORN 0–3 MONTHS
3.5–4 heads in length

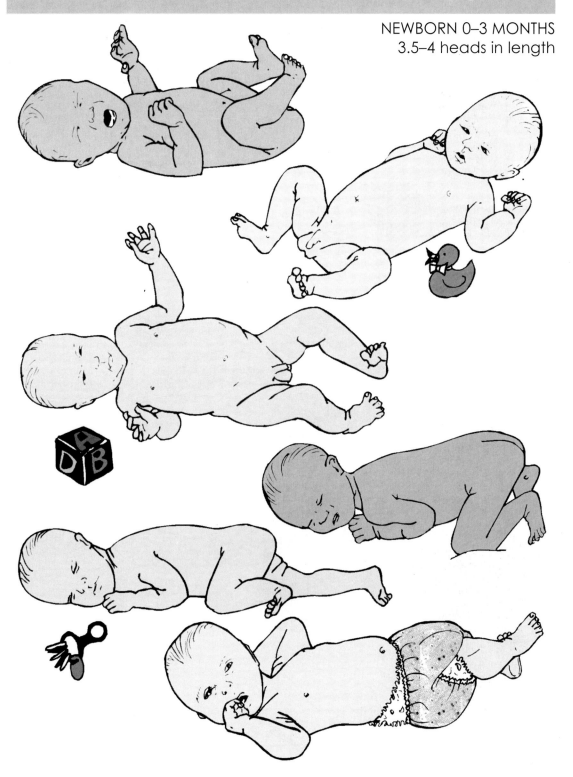

3–9 MONTHS
4 heads in length

4 figures

12–14 MONTHS
4 heads in height

14–20 MONTHS
4 heads in height

20–24 MONTHS
4 heads in height

2–2½ YEARS
4 heads in height

2½–4 YEARS
4–4.5 heads in height

2½–4 YEARS
4–4.5 heads in height

5–6 YEARS
4.5 heads in height

5–6 YEARS
4.5 heads in height

7–9 YEARS
5 heads in height

7–9 YEARS
5 heads in height

7–9 YEARS
5 heads in height

10–11 YEARS
5.5 heads in height

10–11 YEARS
5.5 heads in height

12–14 YEARS
6 heads in height

12–14 YEARS
6 heads in height

12–14 YEARS
6 heads in height

12–14 YEARS
6 heads in height

MIDDLE MARKET
HIGH STREET
STREET LEVEL

MIDDLE MARKET
HIGH STREET
STREET LEVEL

MIDDLE MARKET
HIGH STREET
STREET LEVEL

MIDDLE MARKET
HIGH STREET
STREET LEVEL

TEENAGE MARKET

TEENAGE MARKET

TEENAGE MARKET

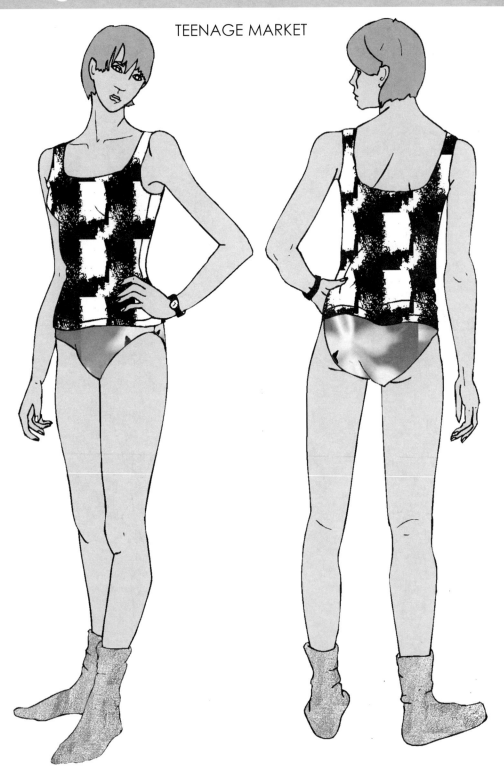

TEENAGE MARKET

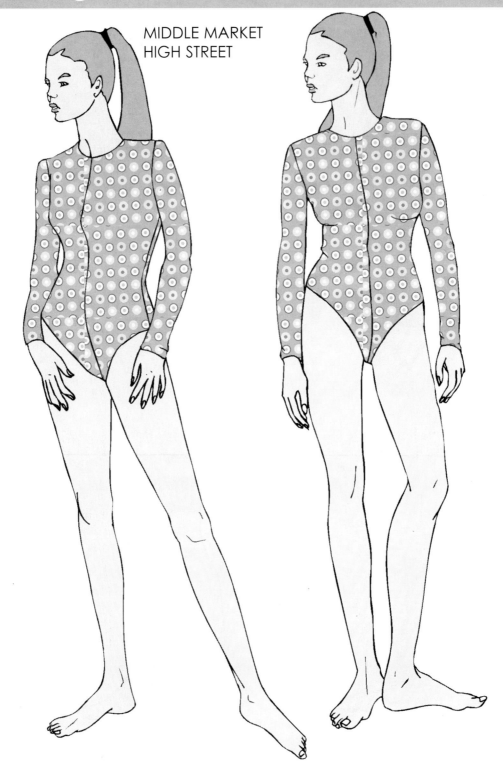

MIDDLE MARKET
HIGH STREET

MIDDLE MARKET
HIGH STREET

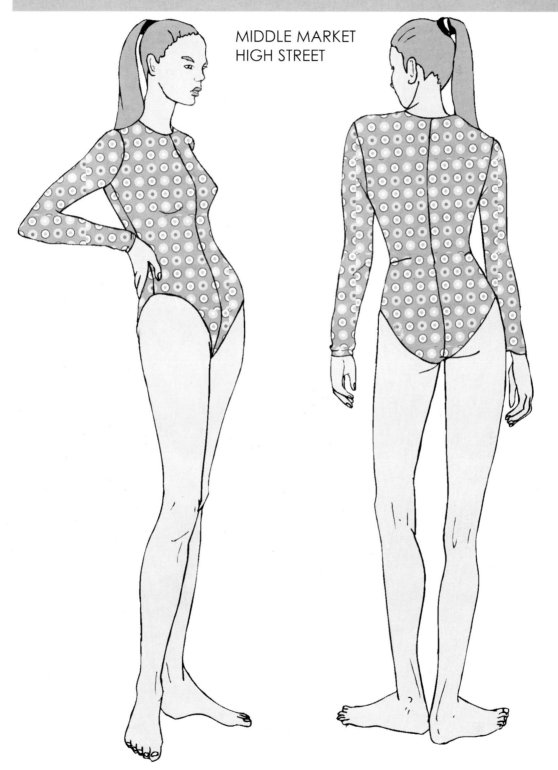

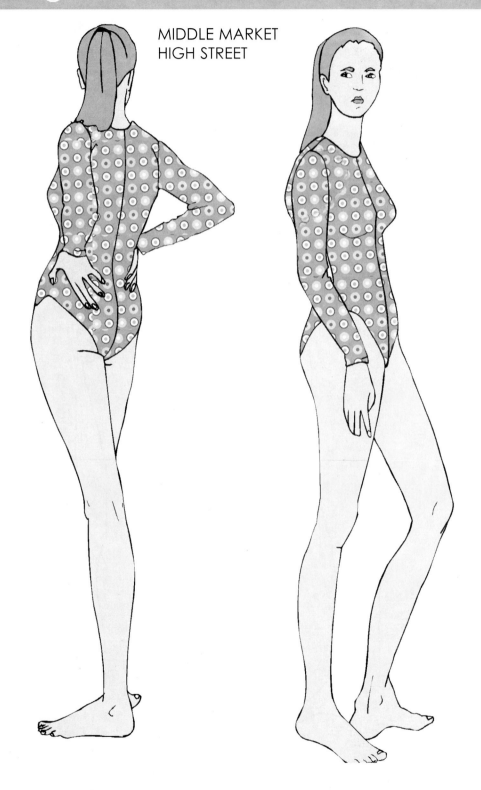

MIDDLE MARKET
HIGH STREET

MIDDLE MARKET
HIGH STREET

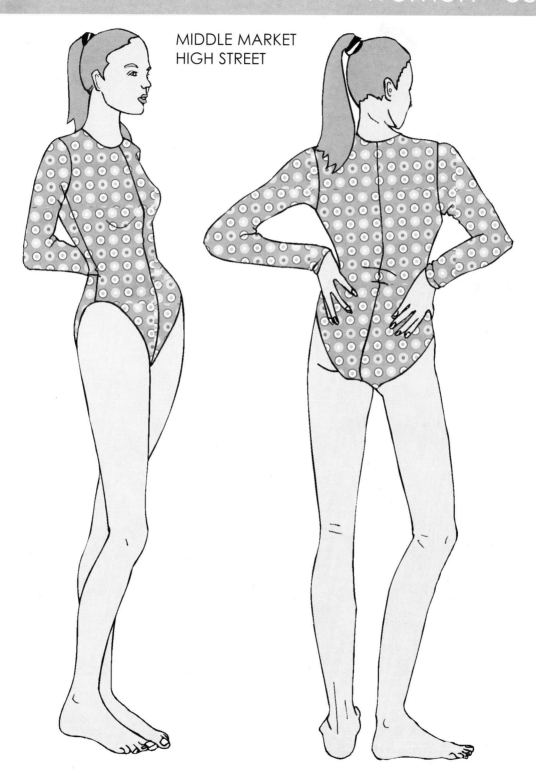

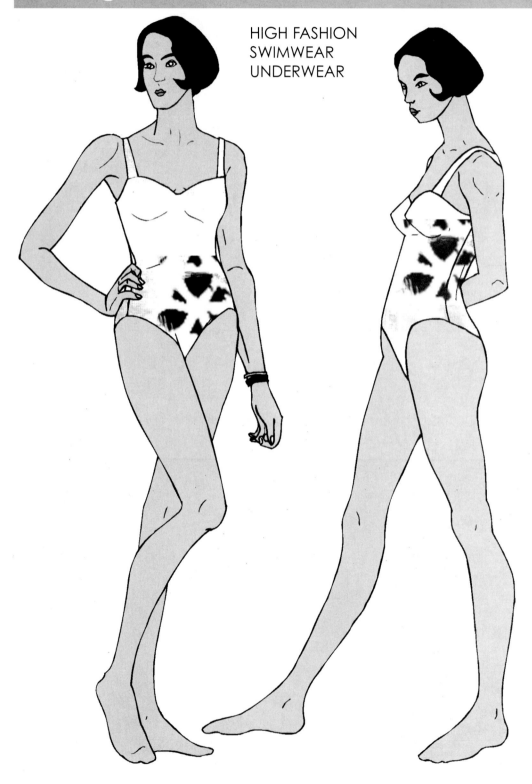

HIGH FASHION
SWIMWEAR
UNDERWEAR

HIGH FASHION
SWIMWEAR
UNDERWEAR

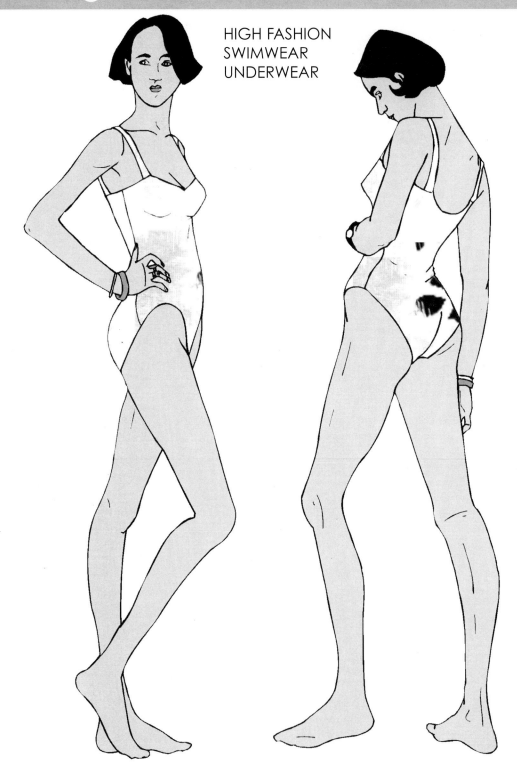

HIGH FASHION
SWIMWEAR
UNDERWEAR

HIGH FASHION
SWIMWEAR
UNDERWEAR

MIDDLE MARKET
STREET LEVEL

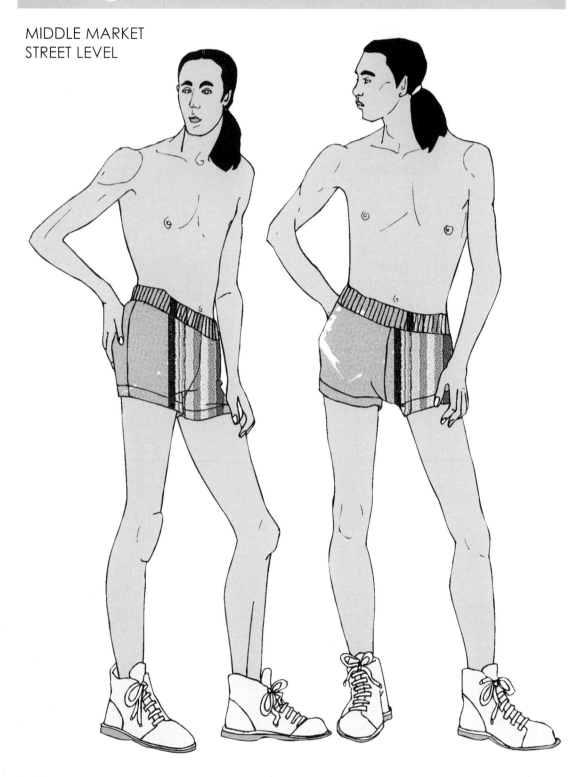

MIDDLE MARKET
STREET LEVEL

MIDDLE MARKET
STREET LEVEL

MIDDLE MARKET
STREET LEVEL

HIGH FASHION
HIGH STREET FASHION

HIGH FASHION
HIGH STREET FASHION

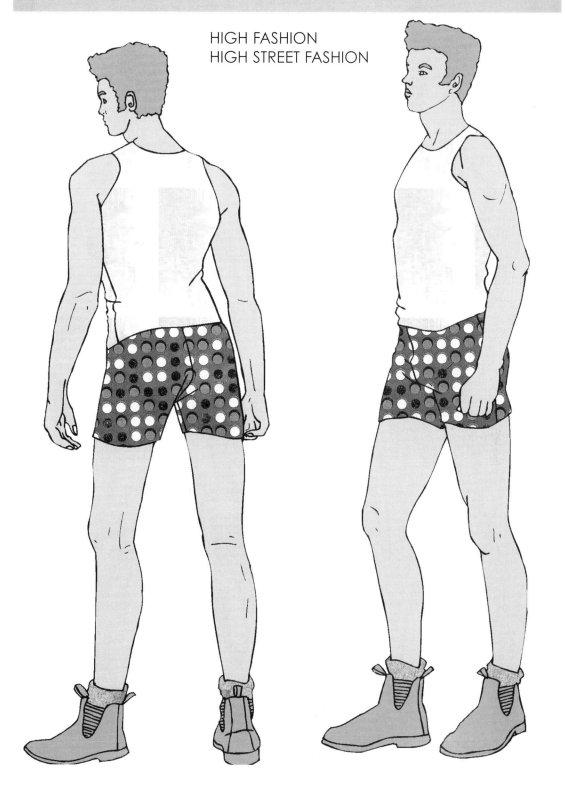

HIGH FASHION
HIGH STREET FASHION

HIGH FASHION
HIGH STREET FASHION

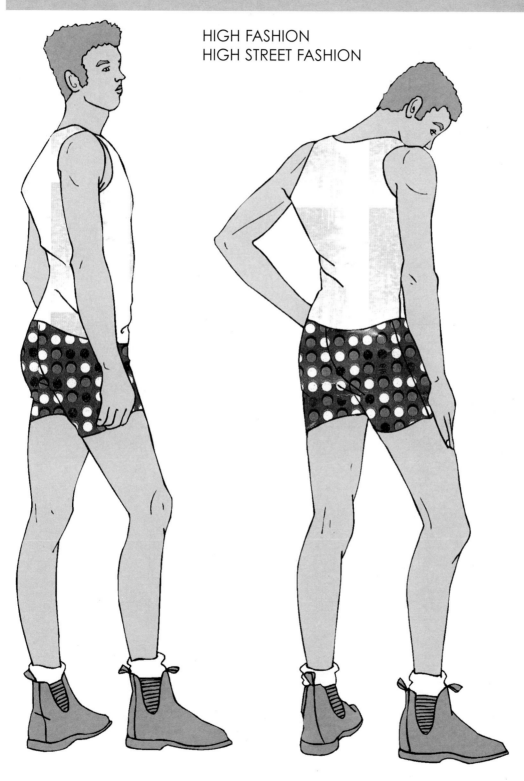

HIGH FASHION
HIGH STREET FASHION

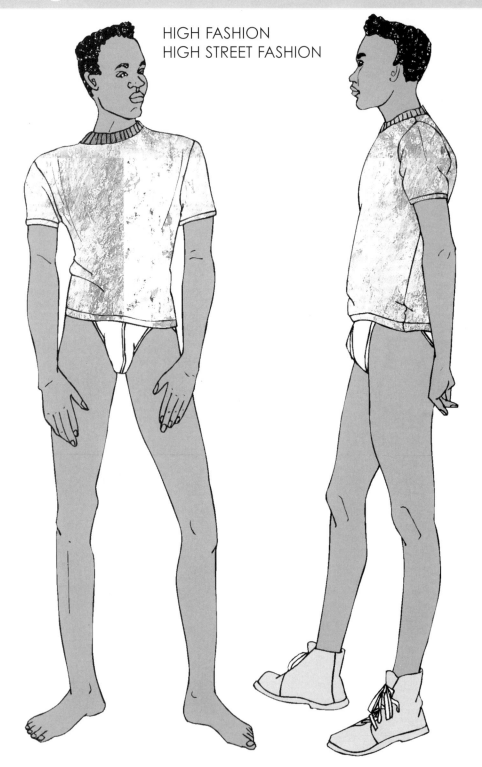

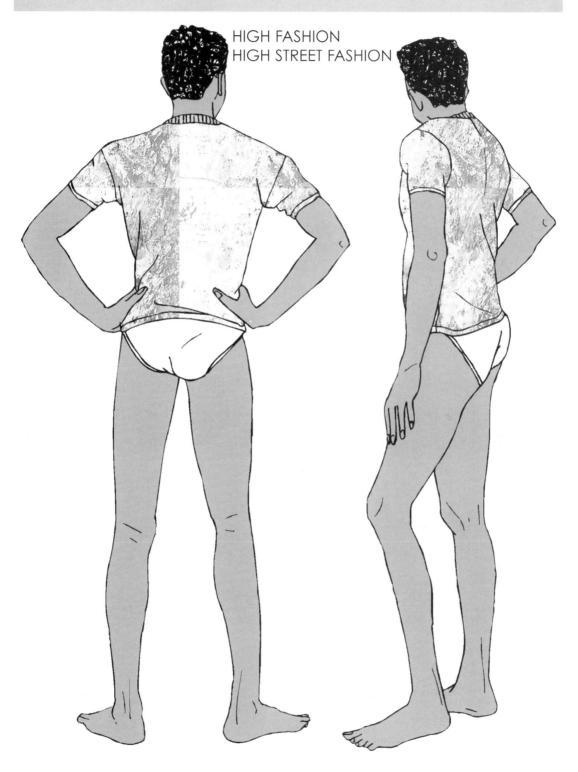

HIGH FASHION
HIGH STREET FASHION

HIGH FASHION
HIGH STREET FASHION

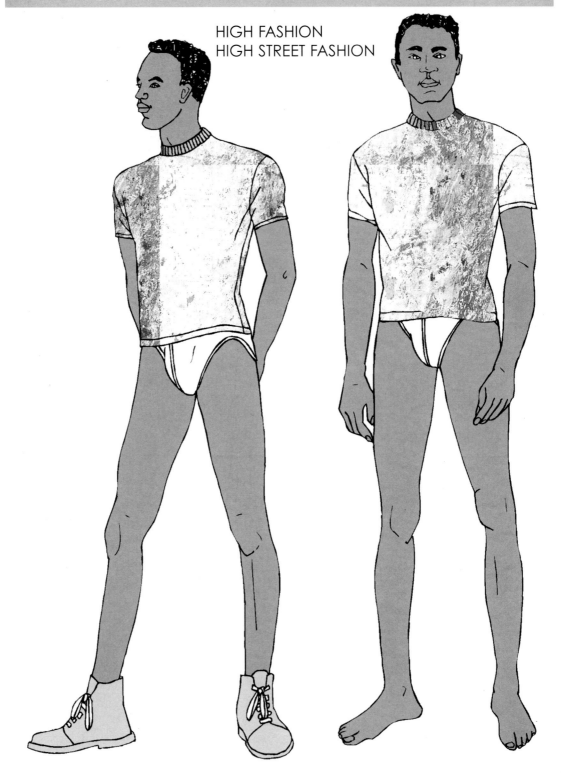

HIGH FASHION
HIGH STREET FASHION

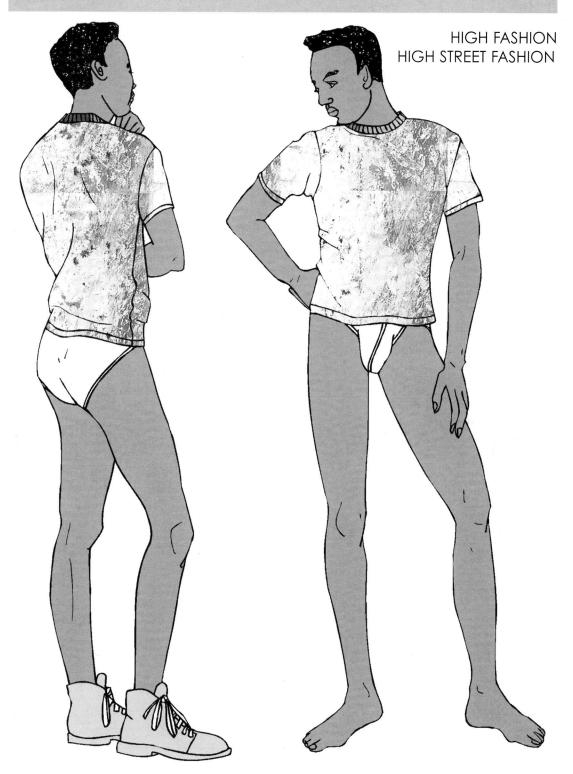

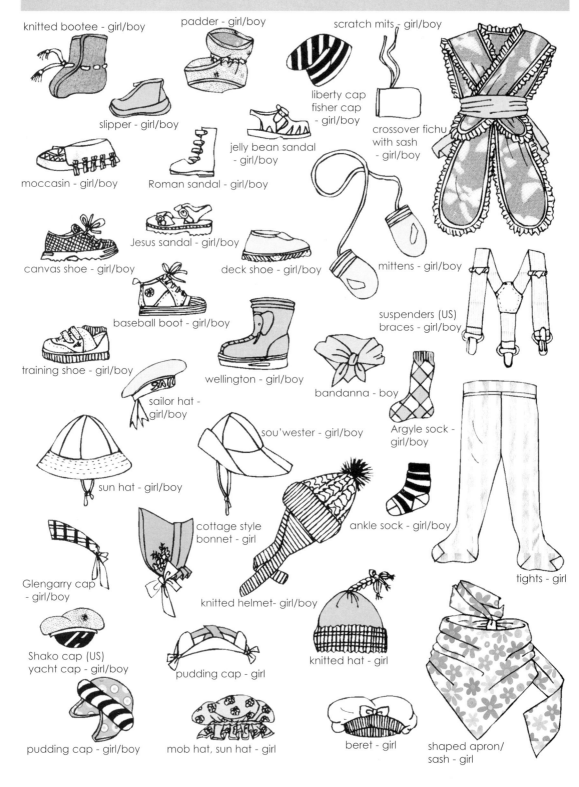

knitted bootee - girl/boy

padder - girl/boy

scratch mits - girl/boy

slipper - girl/boy

liberty cap
fisher cap
- girl/boy

jelly bean sandal
- girl/boy

crossover fichu
with sash
- girl/boy

moccasin - girl/boy

Roman sandal - girl/boy

Jesus sandal - girl/boy

deck shoe - girl/boy

mittens - girl/boy

canvas shoe - girl/boy

baseball boot - girl/boy

suspenders (US)
braces - girl/boy

training shoe - girl/boy

wellington - girl/boy

bandanna - boy

sailor hat -
girl/boy

sou'wester - girl/boy

Argyle sock -
girl/boy

sun hat - girl/boy

cottage style
bonnet - girl

ankle sock - girl/boy

Glengarry cap
- girl/boy

knitted helmet- girl/boy

tights - girl

Shako cap (US)
yacht cap - girl/boy

pudding cap - girl

knitted hat - girl

pudding cap - girl/boy

mob hat, sun hat - girl

beret - girl

shaped apron/
sash - girl

vest with poppers - girl/boy

liberty bodice - girl/boy

corded stays - girl/boy

bodysuit - girl

all-in-one vest - girl/boy

plastic pants - girl/boy

vest - girl/boy

bib - girl/boy

pants - boy
briefs - girls

night drawers
night suit
sleeper - girl/boy

Babygro™
stretch coverall - girl/boy

apron bib - girl/boy
side view

swimsuit - girl

underskirt - girl

petticoat - girl

bib with sleeves - girl/boy

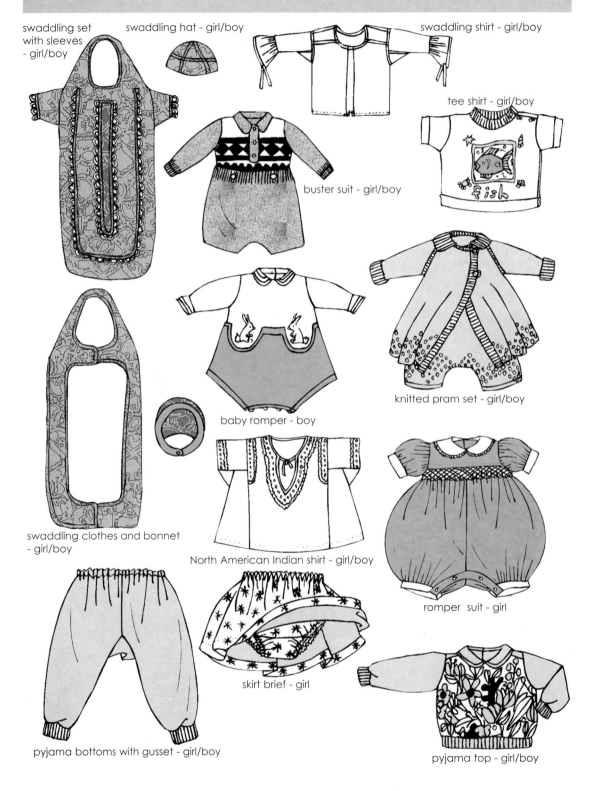

swaddling set
with sleeves
- girl/boy

swaddling hat - girl/boy

swaddling shirt - girl/boy

tee shirt - girl/boy

buster suit - girl/boy

baby romper - boy

knitted pram set - girl/boy

swaddling clothes and bonnet
- girl/boy

North American Indian shirt - girl/boy

romper suit - girl

pyjama bottoms with gusset - girl/boy

skirt brief - girl

pyjama top - girl/boy

leggings - girl

baby jeans - girl/boy

jumper (US)
pinafore - girl

kilt - girl

dungaree dress - girl

all-over apron - girl

jumper (US)
pinafore - girl

apron with Betsie
collar - girl

drill dress, gymslip - girl

pinafore and
guimpe - girl

jumpsuit - boy

brownie suit (US)
overalls - boy

drawers - girl

dungarees - girl/boy

bathing suit - boy

Turkish trousers
bloomers - girl

bathing suit - girl

cardigan - girl/boy

matinée jacket - girl/boy

embroidered shawl
- girl/boy

hussar tunic - boy

Figaro jacket/suit - girl

christening robe - girl/boy

dress with pantaloons - girl

christening bonnet and
shoes - girl/boy

Norfolk suit - girl

Kate Greenaway inspired dress - girl

nightgown - girl/boy

princess dress
(draped) - girl

fishwife draped overskirt - girl

overdress
(velvet) - girl

princess dress
(sashed) - girl

slip/baby dress - girl/boy

shepherd's smock
- girl/boy

baby's pelisse - girl/boy

dress and pant - girl

sailor suit - girl

reefer suit - girl

Little Lord Fauntleroy suit - boy

tunic and trousers - boy

Buster Brown suit (US)
Russian suit
military blouse - boy

Zouave suit - boy

Eton collar suit - boy

skeleton suit - boy

skeleton suit with ruff - boy

baby's skeleton suit - boy

Norfolk suit - boy

young boy's suit - boy

school boy's suit - boy

sailor suit - boy

Garibaldi suit - boy

oilskin
plastic mackintosh - girl/boy

Montgomery
duffle coat
- girl/boy

showerproof coat - girl/boy

djellabah
- girl/boy

hooded anorak - girl/boy

sleeping bag
shelter bag
- girl/boy

Korean child's jacket - girl/boy

carrying cape - girl/boy

hooded circular cloak
with ball fringe - girl

scalloped cloak
sack - girl/boy

Korean dress - girl/boy

Siberian anorak - girl/boy

highwayman coat -
girl/boy

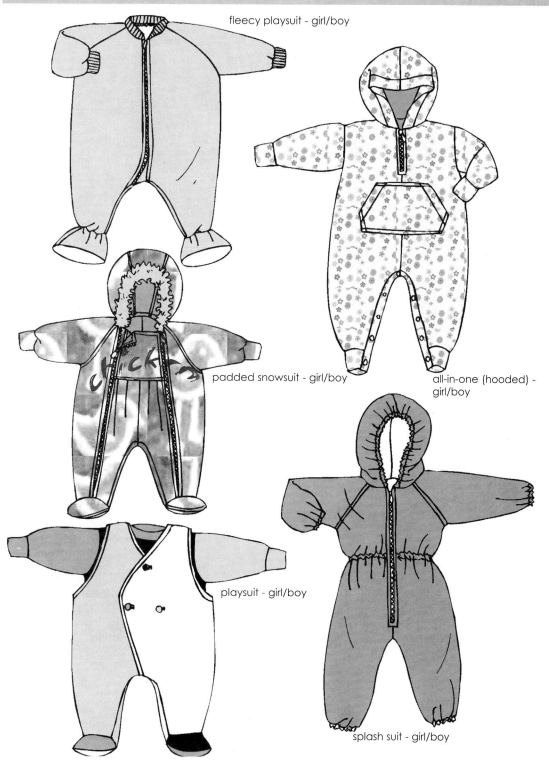

fleecy playsuit - girl/boy

padded snowsuit - girl/boy

all-in-one (hooded) - girl/boy

playsuit - girl/boy

splash suit - girl/boy

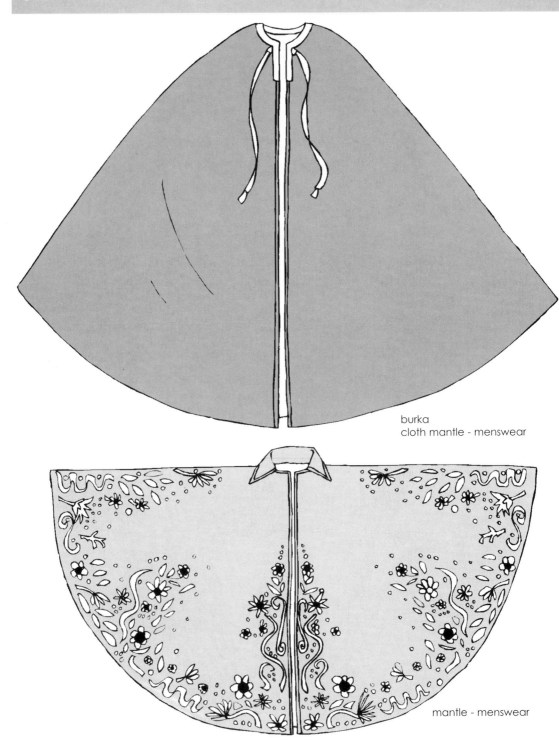

burka
cloth mantle - menswear

mantle - menswear

cape with buttons - menswear

djellabah - menswear

garde de corps with hanging sleeves - menswear

poncho cape (hooded) - menswear

box coat
coachman's coat -
menswear

incroyable coat -
menswear

cut-away coat - menswear

polonaise style coat with
Brandenburg fastenings -
menswear

tail coat -
menswear

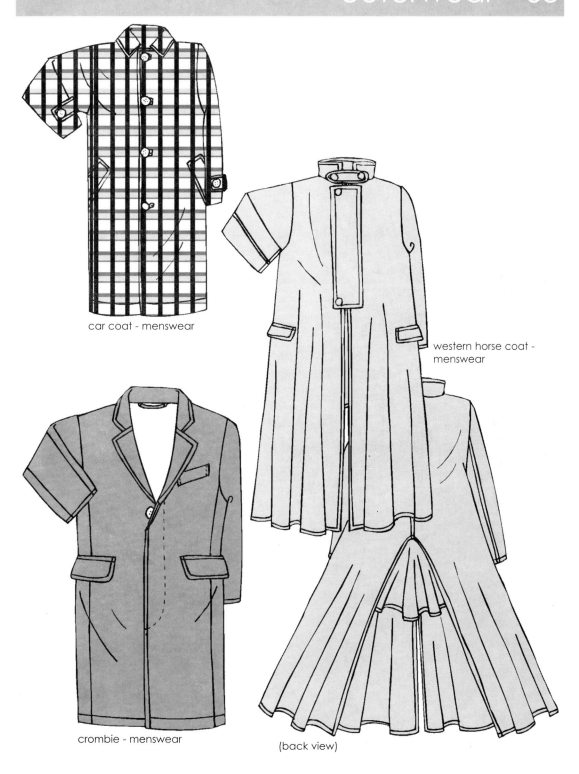

car coat - menswear

western horse coat - menswear

crombie - menswear

(back view)

classic 1960s - womenswear

1920s coat - womenswear

early motoring coat - womenswear

Afghan - mens/womenswear

(front)

(back)

kimono - mens/womenswear

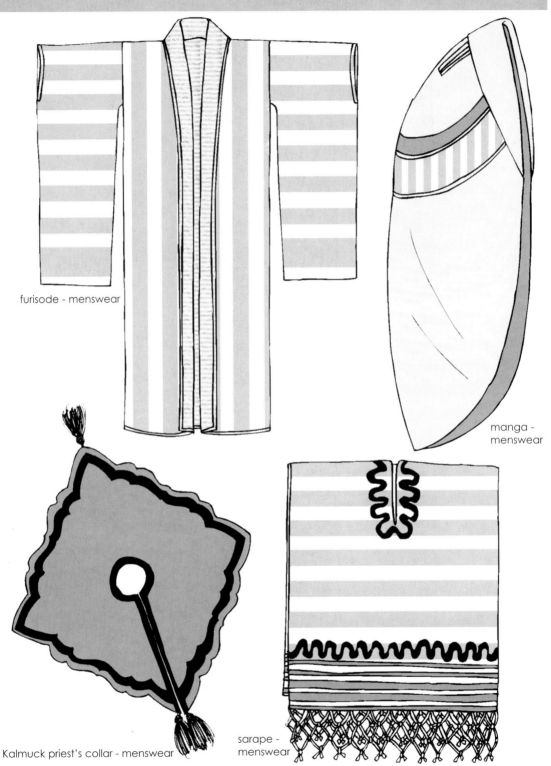

furisode - menswear

manga - menswear

Kalmuck priest's collar - menswear

sarape - menswear

capothe - menswear

Siberian hooded coat - menswear

Siberian smock - menswear

burka and mesh eye-piece
chadri -
womenswear

hayk - menswear

pelisse - womenswear

witchoura - womenswear

paletot - womenswear

half redingote - womenswear

cocoon - womenswear

redingote - womenswear

goller - womenswear

visite - womenswear

slicker - mens/womenswear

steamer coat - mens/womenswear

short fitted coat - womenswear

princess line coat - womenswear

duster - womenswear

swagger - womenswear

A-line coat - womenswear

wrapover/clutch - womenswear

(back view)

Yakut woman's apron and coat - womenswear

(apron)

heuke with hat - womenswear

(back view)

mantelet (fur trimmed) - menswear

ropa
vlieger
marlotte - womenswear

medieval cloak (hooded) - mens/womenswear

cape - mens/womenswear

hoike - menswear

balmacaan - menswear

abayeh
aba - menswear

Taglioni coat - menswear

Inverness cloak - menswear

(back view)

academic
gown -
mens/
womenswear

shoulder cape coat - menswear

trench coat - mens/womenswear

frock coat - menswear

Chesterfield - menswear

cycle mac - mens/womenswear

loden - mens/womenswear

Ulster - mens/womenswear

mackintosh - mens/
womenswear

Ulster (back view)

duffle
Montgomery -
mens/womenswear

gabardine raincoat - mens/womenswear

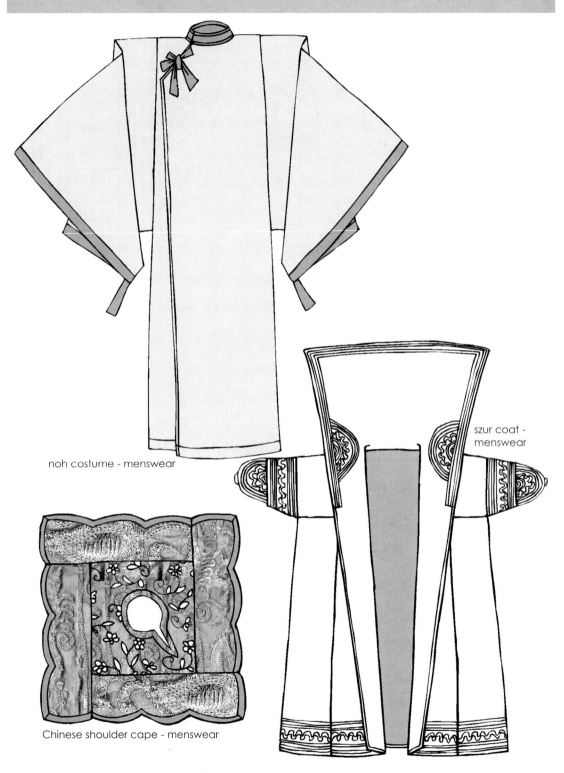

noh costume - menswear

szur coat - menswear

Chinese shoulder cape - menswear

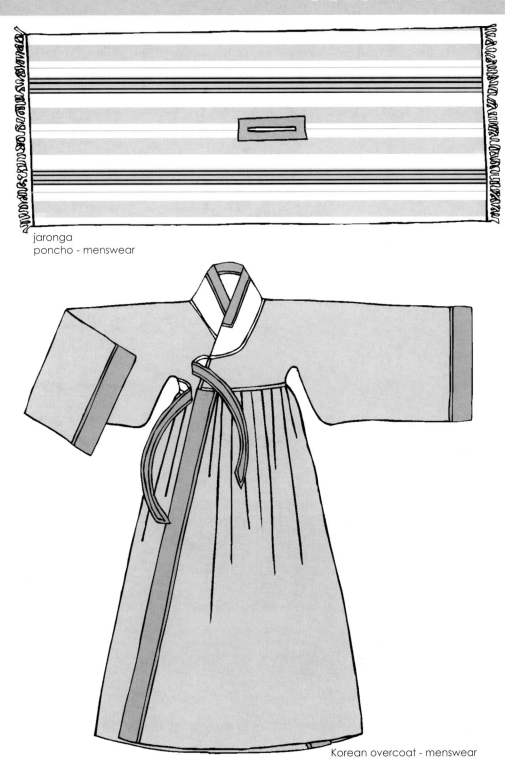

jaronga
poncho - menswear

Korean overcoat - menswear

double-
breasted -
mens/womens
wear
(woman's
fastening)

Spencer -
womenswear

basque - womenswear

bolero - mens/womenswear

single-breasted -
mens/womenswear
(woman's fastening)

casual jacket - womenswear

blazer - mens/womenswear
(woman's cut)

maternity - womenswear

John Galliano jacket -
womenswear

shawl -
womenswear

cape - womenswear

caraco - womenswear

cardigan jacket - womenswear

stole - womenswear

caraco - womenswear (side view)

hussar - womenswear

pashmina - womenswear

peplum - womenswear

canezou - womenswear

Tyrolean loden - mens/womenswear

hacking riding - mens/womenswear

tippet - womenswear

Chanel - womenswear box - mens/womenswear

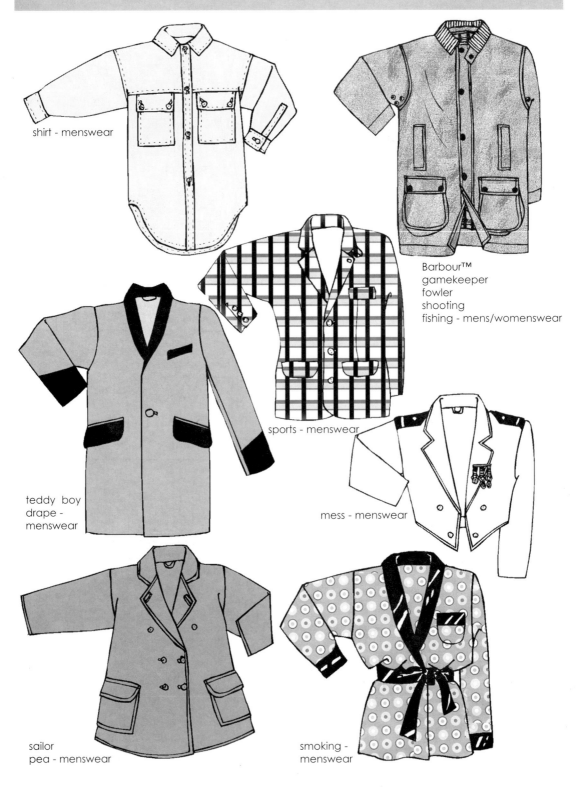

shirt - menswear

Barbour™
gamekeeper
fowler
shooting
fishing - mens/womenswear

sports - menswear

teddy boy
drape -
menswear

mess - menswear

sailor
pea - menswear

smoking -
menswear

denim - mens/womenswear

naval reefer - menswear

camouflage smock
combat - menswear

bomber - mens/womenswear

gas jacket - mens/womenswear

biker - mens/womenswear

Chinese workwear -
mens/womenswear

continental sack coat
(man's fastening) - menswear

capelet - womenswear

embroidered - menswear

Ivy League - menswear

tuxedo - menswear

waiter's - menswear

carmagnole - menswear

sack coat - menswear

bell boy (US)
page boy - menswear

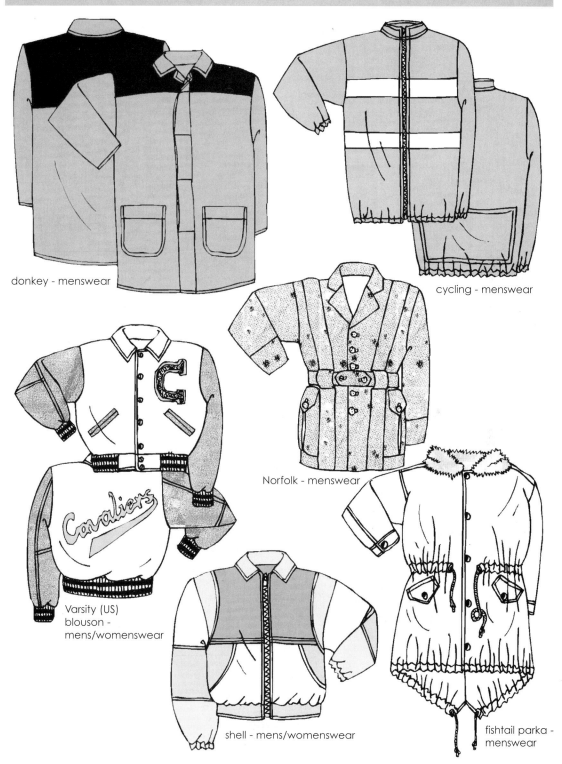

donkey - menswear

cycling - menswear

Norfolk - menswear

Varsity (US)
blouson -
mens/womenswear

shell - mens/womenswear

fishtail parka -
menswear

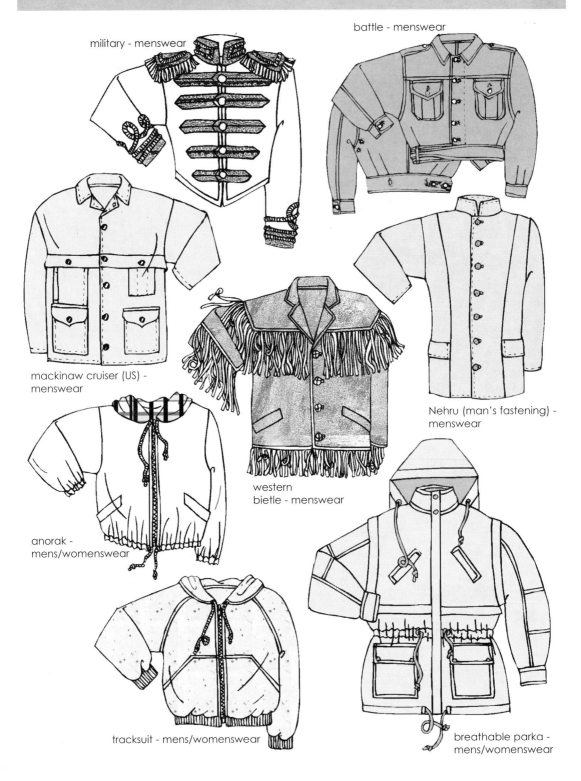

military - menswear

battle - menswear

mackinaw cruiser (US) -
menswear

Nehru (man's fastening) -
menswear

western
bietle - menswear

anorak -
mens/womenswear

tracksuit - mens/womenswear

breathable parka -
mens/womenswear

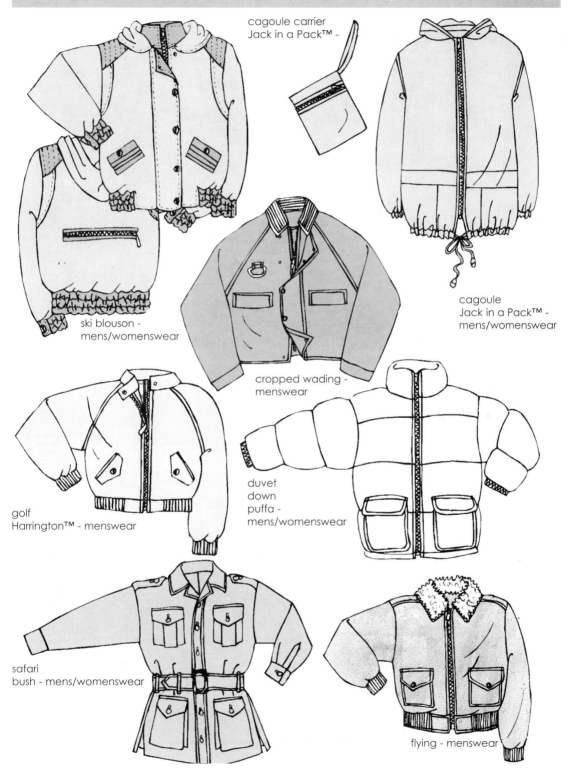

cagoule carrier
Jack in a Pack™ -

ski blouson -
mens/womenswear

cagoule
Jack in a Pack™ -
mens/womenswear

cropped wading -
menswear

golf
Harrington™ - menswear

duvet
down
puffa -
mens/womenswear

safari
bush - mens/womenswear

flying - menswear

tschepken - menswear

gheila
Tunisian man's - menswear

Colley Westonward -
menswear

cotehardie -
mens/womenswear

Mandilion - menswear

Burmese jacket - womenswear

shober - menswear

Siberian man's - menswear

kamishimo - menswear

poncho - mens/
womenswear

grossera skin coat - menswear

aba - menswear

tabard - menswear

surcoat - mens/womenswear

under doublet - menswear

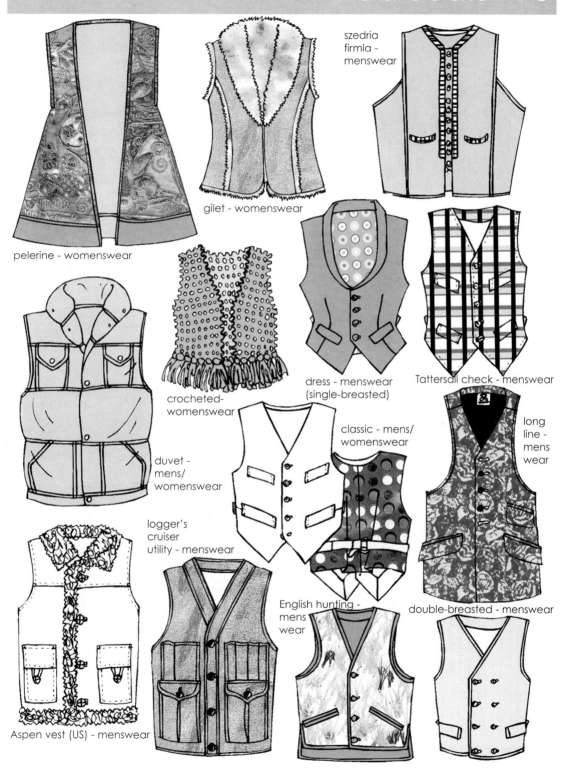

pelerine - womenswear

gilet - womenswear

szedria firmla - menswear

crocheted- womenswear

dress - menswear (single-breasted)

Tattersall check - menswear

duvet - mens/ womenswear

classic - mens/ womenswear

long line - mens wear

logger's cruiser utility - menswear

English hunting - mens wear

double-breasted - menswear

Aspen vest (US) - menswear

hot pants - womenswear

jogging - mens/womens wear

pleated shorts with turn-ups - mens/womens wear

jams (US) - menswear

rehearsal shorts - womenswear

cycling shorts - menswear

trunk hose and cannons/canions - menswear

eight panel cycling shorts - mens/womenswear

lederhosen - menswear

short shorts - womenswear

beach bloomers - womenswear

shorts with built in briefs - menswear

hipsters - womenswear

slashed trunk hose - menswear

shorts skirt - womenswear

culottes - womenswear

athletic shorts with bib - menswear

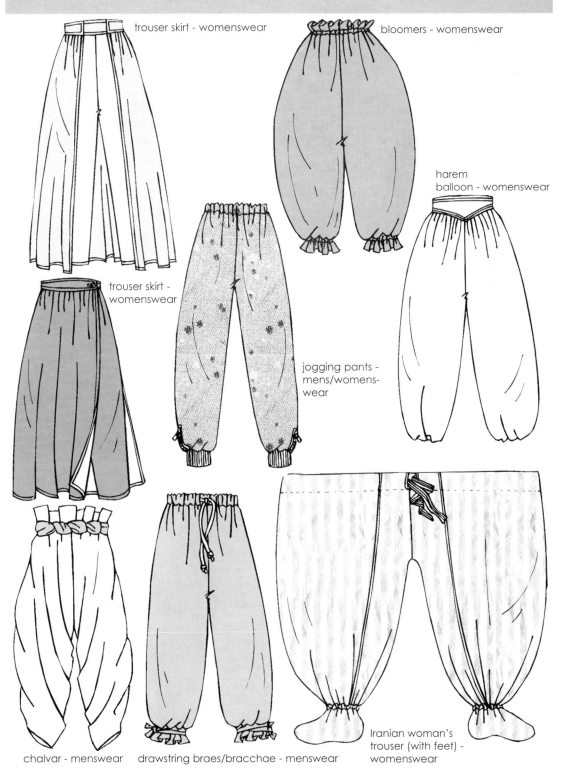

trouser skirt - womenswear

bloomers - womenswear

harem
balloon - womenswear

trouser skirt -
womenswear

jogging pants -
mens/womens-
wear

chalvar - menswear

drawstring braes/bracchae - menswear

Iranian woman's
trouser (with feet) -
womenswear

gaucho - womenswear

palazzo - womenswear

hot pants with bib - womenswear

woman's worksuit - womenswear

body suit catsuit - womenswear

straight tailored - mens/womenswear

leggings - womenswear

capri - womenswear

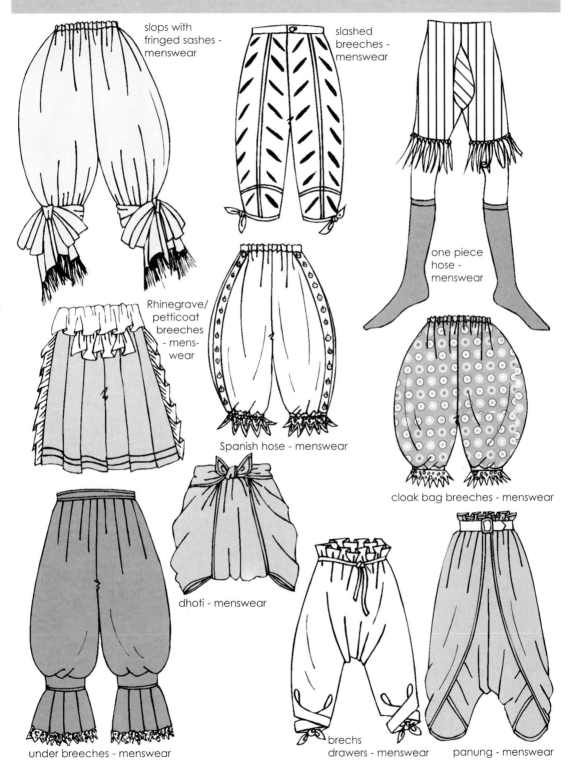

slops with
fringed sashes -
menswear

slashed
breeches -
menswear

one piece
hose -
menswear

Rhinegrave/
petticoat
breeches
- mens-
wear

Spanish hose - menswear

cloak bag breeches - menswear

dhoti - menswear

under breeches - menswear

brechs
drawers - menswear

panung - menswear

sans culottes - menswear

pedal pushers - womenswear

Bermudas - menswear

pegged - mens/womenswear

fitted breeches with fall front - menswear

slim jims/drain pipes - mens/womenswear

long knee breeches - menswear

Jamaica shorts -menswear

army fatigues - menswear

toreador - menswear

clam diggers (US) - womenswear

cargo - mens/womenswear

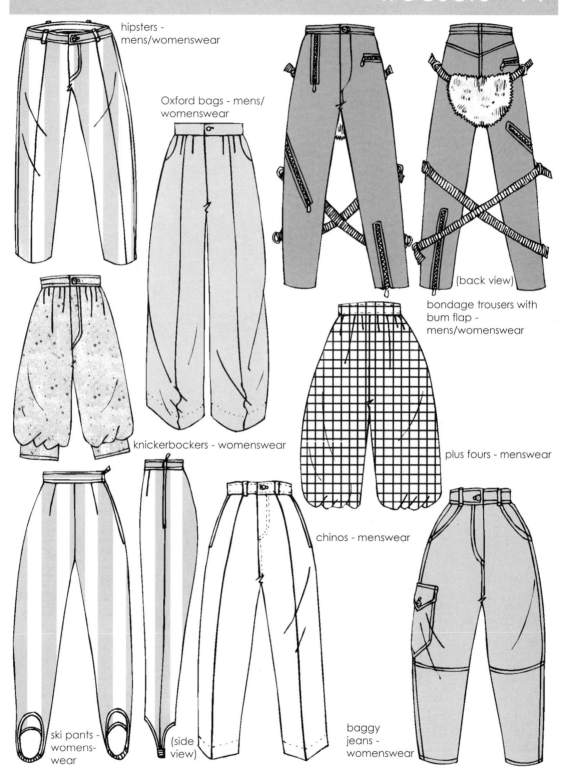

hipsters - mens/womenswear

Oxford bags - mens/womenswear

(back view)

bondage trousers with bum flap - mens/womenswear

knickerbockers - womenswear

plus fours - menswear

chinos - menswear

ski pants - womenswear

(side view)

baggy jeans - womenswear

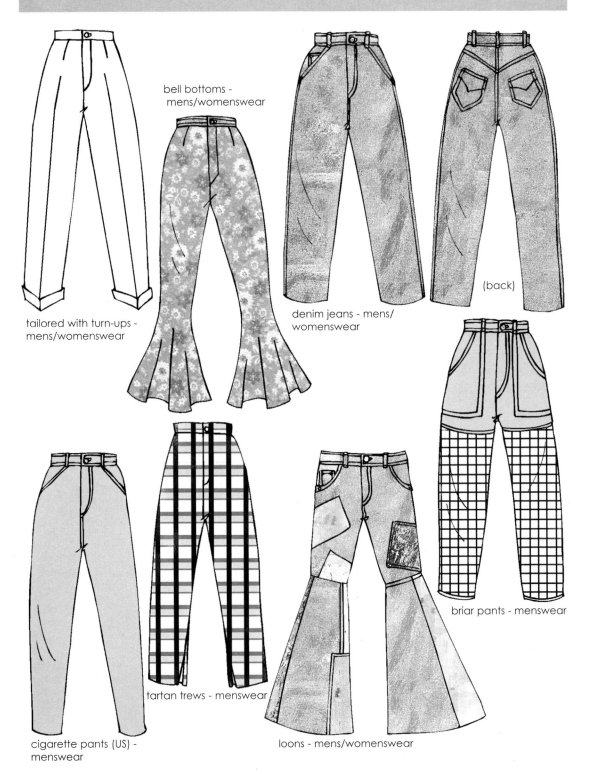

tailored with turn-ups -
mens/womenswear

bell bottoms -
mens/womenswear

denim jeans - mens/
womenswear

(back)

briar pants - menswear

cigarette pants (US) -
menswear

tartan trews - menswear

loons - mens/womenswear

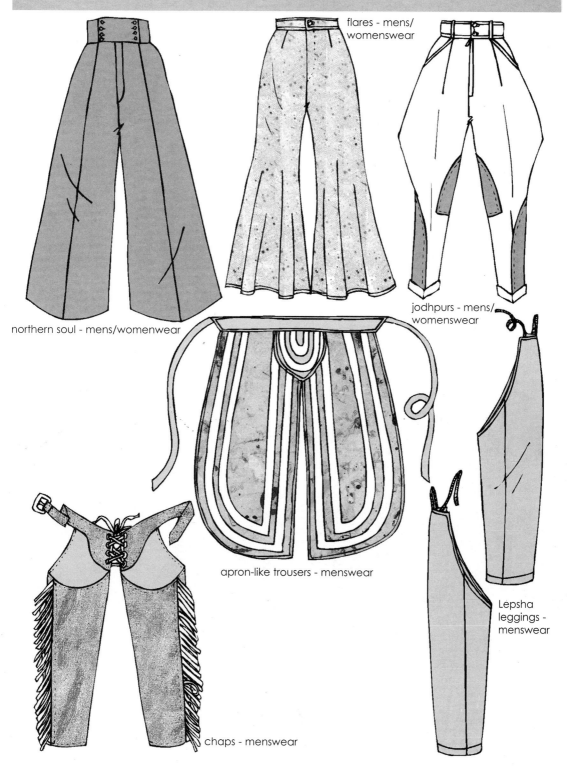

northern soul - mens/womenwear

flares - mens/
womenswear

jodhpurs - mens/
womenswear

apron-like trousers - menswear

chaps - menswear

Lepsha
leggings -
menswear

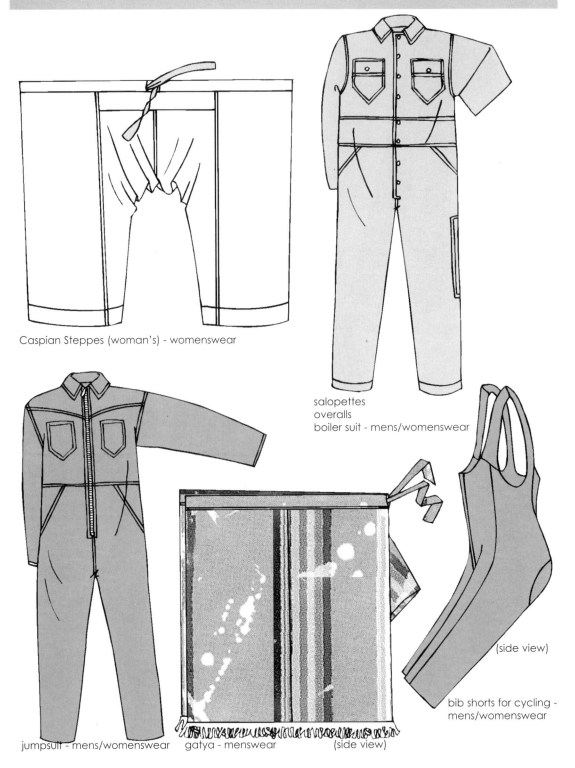

Caspian Steppes (woman's) - womenswear

salopettes
overalls
boiler suit - mens/womenswear

jumpsuit - mens/womenswear   gatya - menswear   (side view)

(side view)

bib shorts for cycling -
mens/womenswear

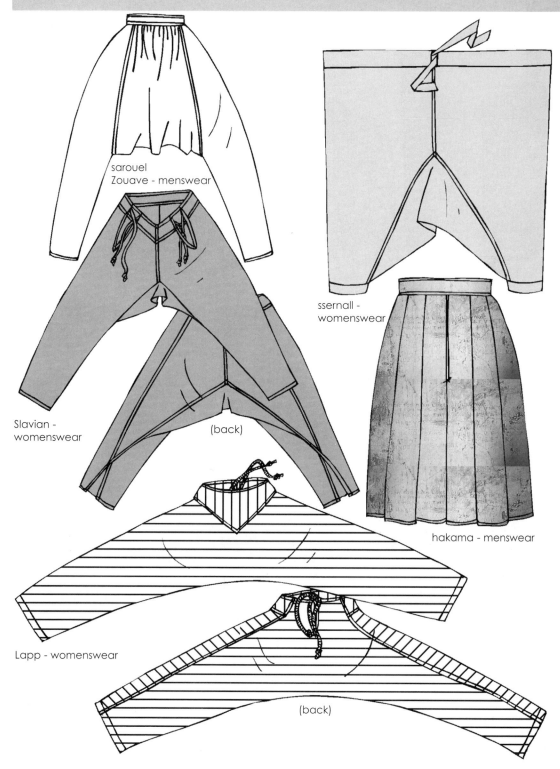

sarouel
Zouave - menswear

ssernall -
womenswear

Slavian -
womenswear

(back)

hakama - menswear

Lapp - womenswear

(back)

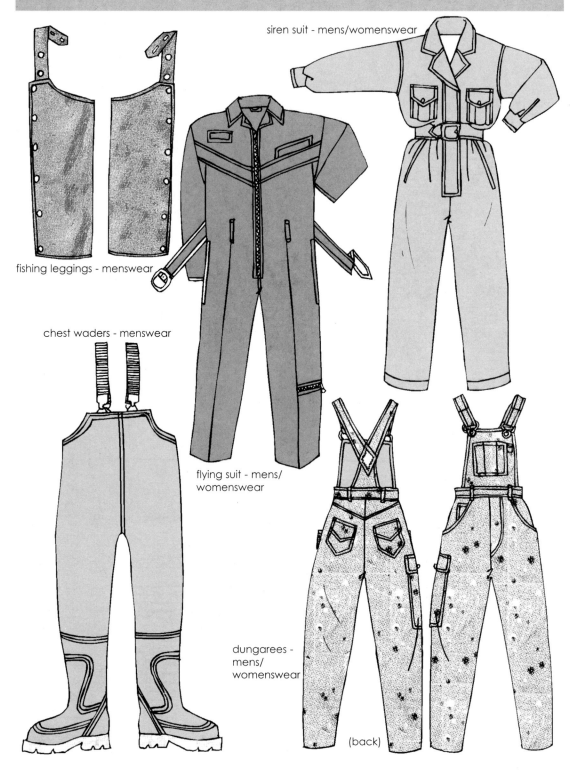

fishing leggings - menswear

siren suit - mens/womenswear

chest waders - menswear

flying suit - mens/womenswear

dungarees - mens/womenswear

(back)

dress - menswear

harlequin - menswear

summer formal - menswear

parti-coloured dress
and harlot - menswear

doublet, breeches and cloak - menswear

catsuit - womenswear

Chesterfield - womenswear

trouser suit - womenswear

Nehru - menswear

zoot - menswear

shell -
mens/womenswear

modern Chanel
suit - womenswear

Chanel -
womenswear

trouser suit -
womenswear

evening
menswear

athletic outfit - womenswear

single-
breasted
two piece -
menswear

micro - womenswear

mini - womenswear

midi - womenswear

maxi - womenswear

floor length
dinner - womenswear

ballerina - womenswear

hobble
pencil - womenswear

flared - womenswear

gored and flared -
womenswear

straight fitted -
womenswear

circular - womenswear

A-line - womenswear

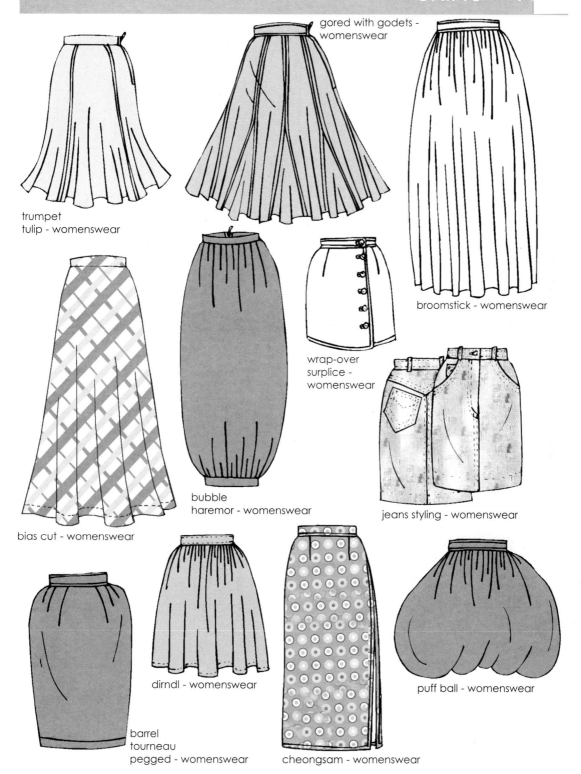

gored with godets -
womenswear

trumpet
tulip - womenswear

broomstick - womenswear

wrap-over
surplice -
womenswear

bias cut - womenswear

bubble
haremor - womenswear

jeans styling - womenswear

barrel
tourneau
pegged - womenswear

dirndl - womenswear

cheongsam - womenswear

puff ball - womenswear

drape and
wrap-over -
womenswear

fishtail - womenswear

handkerchief
hem - womenswear

ire
iro - womenswear

pareo - womenswear

wrap tennis - womenswear

fitted with frill -
womenswear

yoke and gathers -
womenswear

sarong -
womenswear

petal - womenswear

ra-ra -
womens
wear

tiered with ruffles - womenswear

peplum -
womenswear

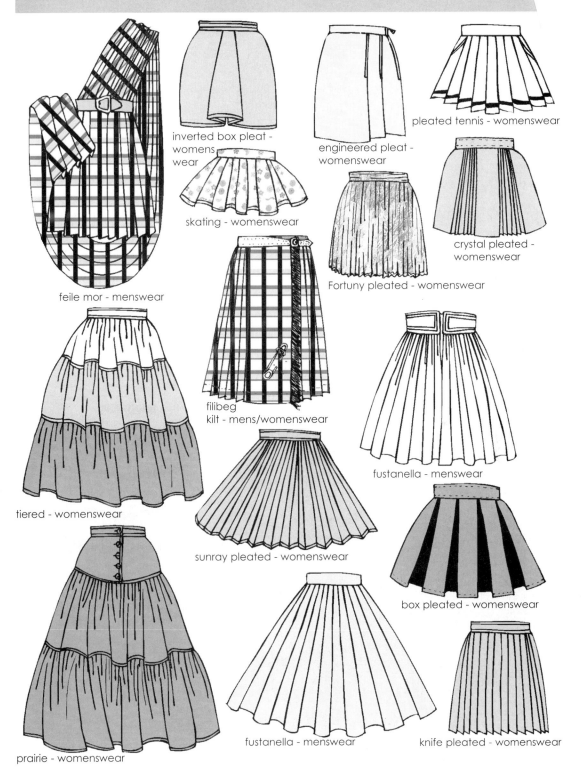

feile mor - menswear

inverted box pleat -
womens
wear

skating - womenswear

engineered pleat -
womenswear

pleated tennis - womenswear

Fortuny pleated - womenswear

crystal pleated -
womenswear

tiered - womenswear

filibeg
kilt - mens/womenswear

fustanella - menswear

sunray pleated - womenswear

box pleated - womenswear

prairie - womenswear

fustanella - menswear

knife pleated - womenswear

hula
grass - mens/womenswear

(side view)

bustle - womenswear

balayeuse
sweeper's - womenswear

(side view)

polonaise - womenswear

(side view)

vertugado with aro - womenswear

tablier
apron with train - womenswear

dress and bloomers - womenswear

two piece - menswear

boxer shorts - menswear

one piece - mens wear

micro bikini - womenswear

bikini - womenswear

trunks - menswear

bloomer suit - womenswear

one piece maillot (US) - womenswear

corset over bloomers - womenswear

4 piece combination bikini - womenswear

1

2

3

4

ballerina suit with trunks - womenswear

sack shift - womens wear

A-line - womenswear

strapless - womenswear

blouson (dropped waist) - womenswear

tiered - womenswear

tent - womenswear

sheath - womenswear

trapeze - womenswear

dropped waist - womenswear

empire line - womenswear

shoulder yoke - womenswear

fit and flare - womenswear

bouffant - womenswear

smock - womenswear

princess line - womenswear

cheongsam - womenswear

shirt - womenswear

wrap-over surplice - womenswear

coat - womenswear

shirt waister - womenswear

cocktail - womenswear

fishtail mumu (US) - womenswear

tabard - womenswear

overall - womenswear

tunic - womenswear

pinafore - womenswear

huipil - womenswear

sarafan - womenswear

(back view)

tutu - womenswear

ballgown - womenswear

ballerina - womenswear

tee shirt dress - womenswear

cotehardie - womenswear

flapper - womenswear

prairie - womenswear

peasant - womenswear

dashiki - womenswear

Indian kurta - womenswear

caftan - womenswear

1940s pannier dress - womenswear

post war dress - womenswear

1960s knitted dress - womenswear

Prom dress - womenswear

1950s floral print dress - womenswear

leg of mutton dress - womenswear

Edwardian dress with train - womenswear

1950s crinoline dress - womenswear

bliaud - womenswear

sacque
sac - womenswear

(back)

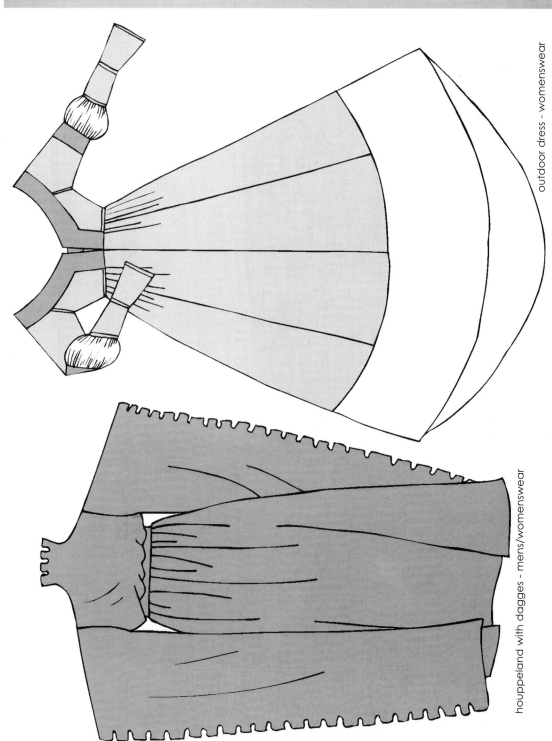

outdoor dress - womenswear

houppeland with dagges - mens/womenswear

toga - menswear

peplos - mens/
womenswear

himation - mens/
womenswear

chiton - womenswear

sari - womenswear

surcoat
surcote -
menswear

dalmatica
with clavi -
menswear

simlah with
tsitsith over
kethoneth -
menswear

cassock - menswear

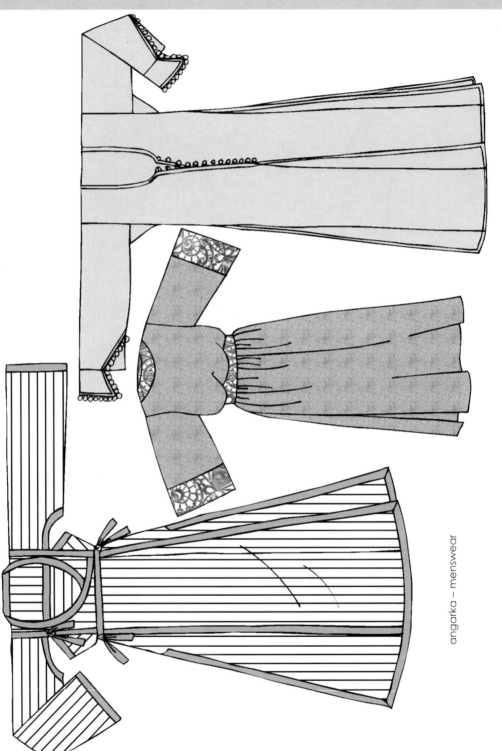

yelek
caftan – womenswear

bliaud – menswear

angarka – menswear

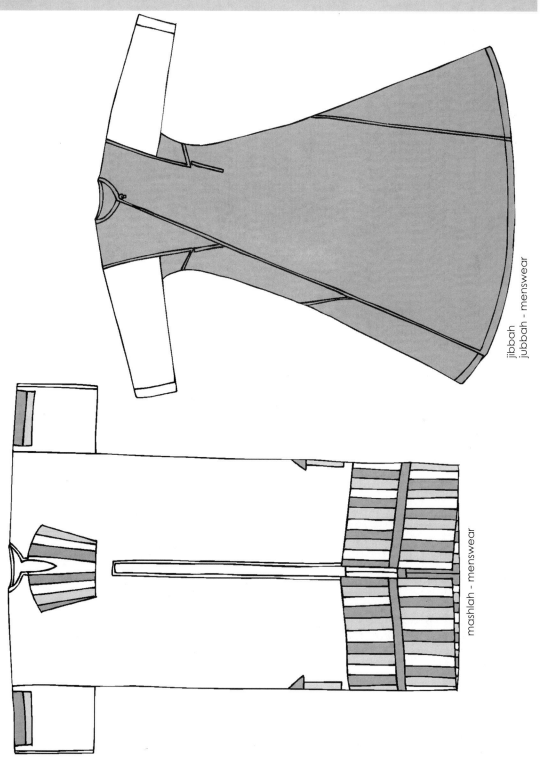

jibbah
jubbah - menswear

mashlah - menswear

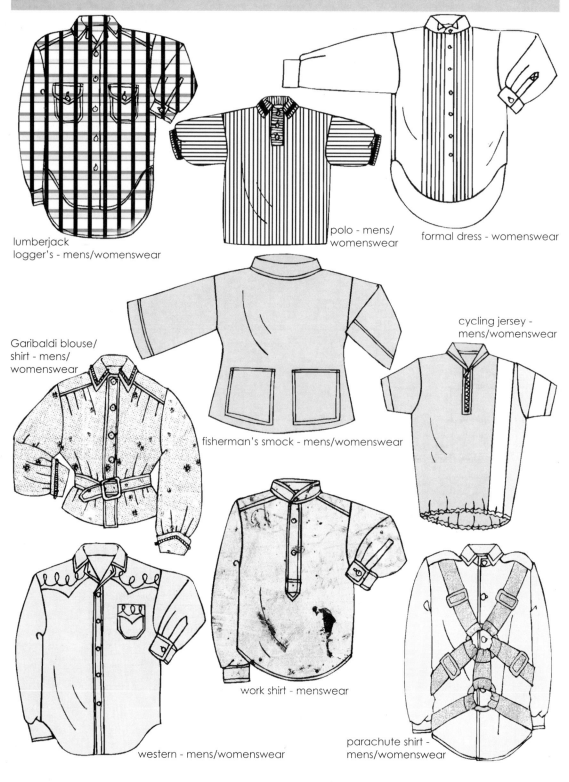

lumberjack
logger's - mens/womenswear

polo - mens/
womenswear

formal dress - womenswear

Garibaldi blouse/
shirt - mens/
womenswear

fisherman's smock - mens/womenswear

cycling jersey -
mens/womenswear

work shirt - menswear

western - mens/womenswear

parachute shirt -
mens/womenswear

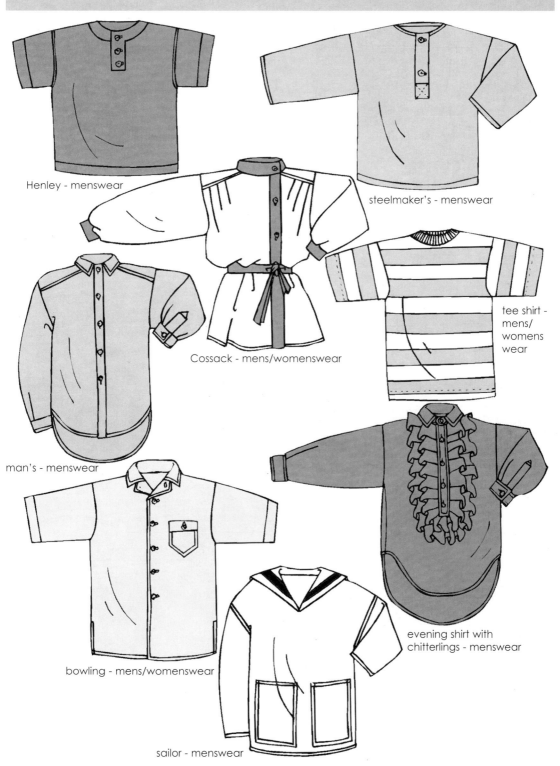

Henley - menswear

steelmaker's - menswear

Cossack - mens/womenswear

tee shirt - mens/ womens wear

man's - menswear

evening shirt with chitterlings - menswear

bowling - mens/womenswear

sailor - menswear

shell blouse - womenswear

princess - womenswear

normal fitted - womenswear

overblouse - womenswear

blouson on yoke - womenswear

ballerina dance - womenswear

bandeau - womenswear

shoulder yoke - womenswear

strapless - womenswear

bustier - womenswear

peasant - womenswear

camisole - womenswear

surplice - womenswear

peasant - womenswear

boob tube - womenswear

casaquin - womens wear

smock - womenswear

petenlair - womenswear

(side views)

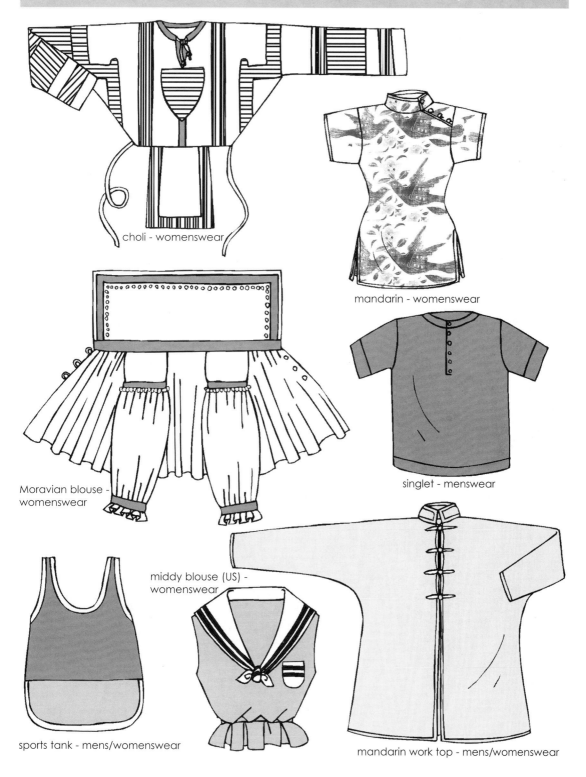

choli - womenswear

mandarin - womenswear

Moravian blouse -
womenswear

singlet - menswear

middy blouse (US) -
womenswear

sports tank - mens/womenswear

mandarin work top - mens/womenswear

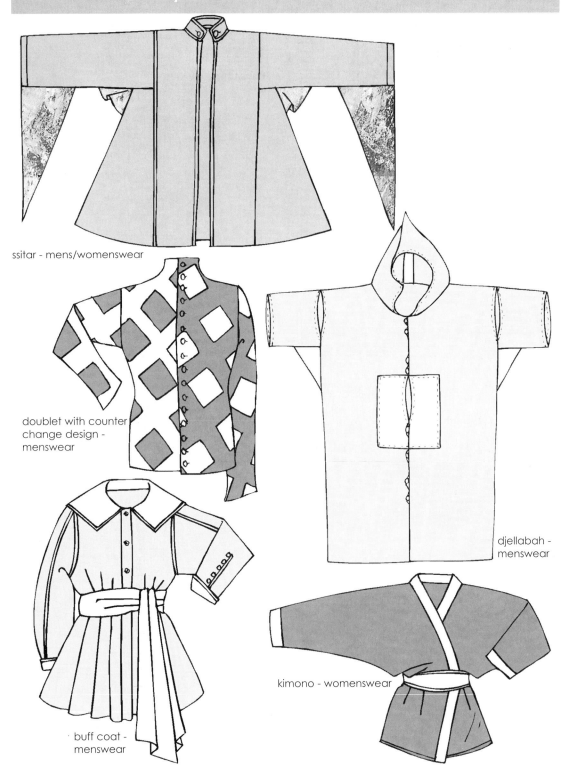

ssitar - mens/womenswear

doublet with counter
change design -
menswear

djellabah -
menswear

buff coat -
menswear

kimono - womenswear

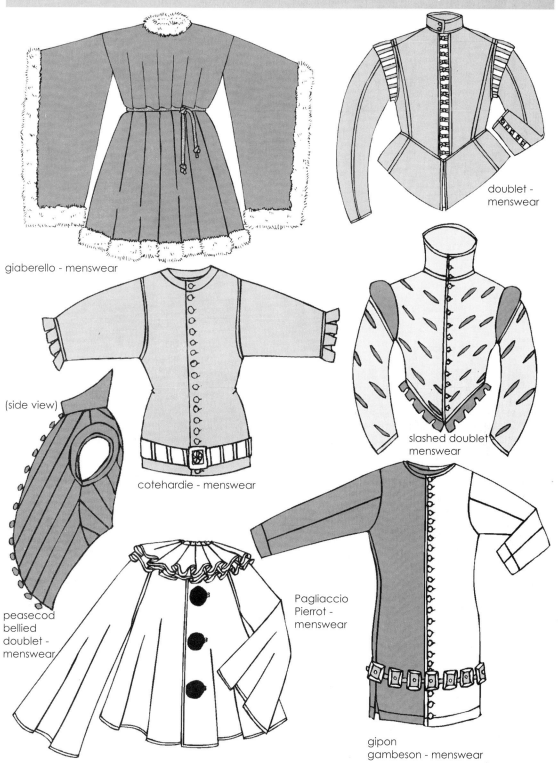

giaberello - menswear

doublet - menswear

(side view)

cotehardie - menswear

slashed doublet menswear

peasecod bellied doublet - menswear

Pagliaccio Pierrot - menswear

gipon gambeson - menswear

boudoir jacket - womenswear

dressing sacque - womenswear

combing jacket
powdering mantle
peignoir - womenswear

hostess coat
house coat - womenswear

negligée - womenswear

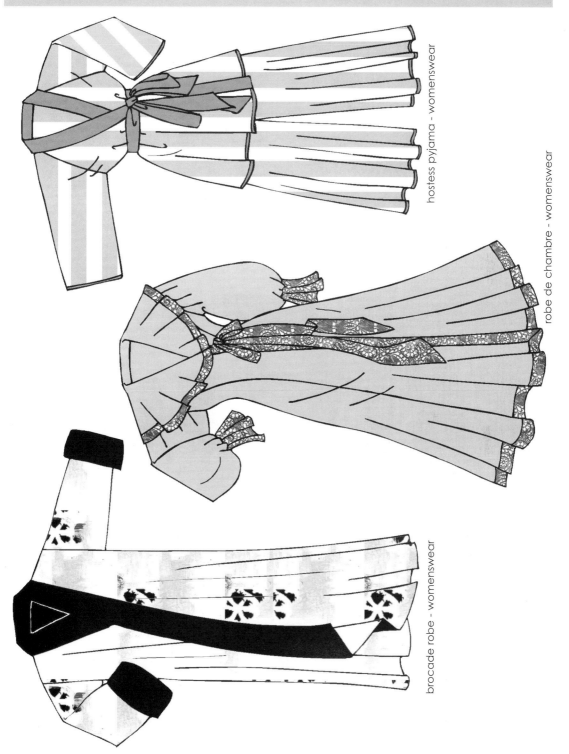

hostess pyjama - womenswear

robe de chambre - womenswear

brocade robe - womenswear

matinée jacket -
womenswear

morning jacket -
womenswear

(back)

kimono - womenswear

lounging pyjamas - womenswear

breakfast cape
bed rayle - womenswear

bed jacket - womenswear

boudoir rayle - womenswear

baby doll's - womenswear

nightgown - womenswear

mandarin sleepcoat - womenswear

night cloak/travelling cloak - womenswear

shortie nightdress - womenswear

bath robe - mens/womenswear

negligée (bias cut) - womenswear

knitted pyjamas - womenswear

striped pyjamas - mens/womenswear

sleepsuit (all-in-one) - menswear

dressing gown - menswear

nightshirt - menswear

sleepcoat - menswear

loose cut pyjamas - womenswear

tee shirt - mens/ womens wear

grandad shirt - mens/ womens- wear

army sweater - menswear

polo shirt - mens/ womens- wear

crew neck pullover sloppy Joe (fully fashioned) - mens/ womenswear

Guernsey - mens/womenswear

cricket sweater - menswear

cut and sew sweatshirt - menswear

punk string knit - mens/womenswear

rugby shirt - menswear

vest - mens/womenswear

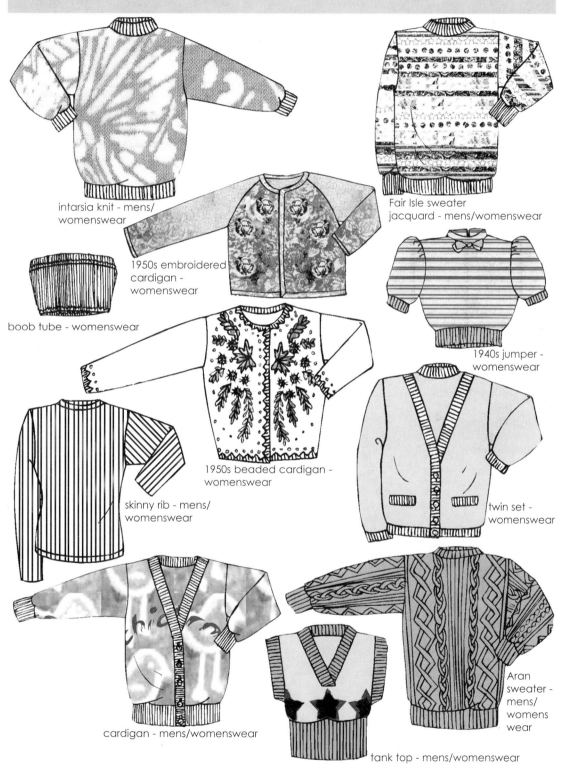

intarsia knit - mens/
womenswear

Fair Isle sweater
jacquard - mens/womenswear

1950s embroidered
cardigan -
womenswear

boob tube - womenswear

1940s jumper -
womenswear

1950s beaded cardigan -
womenswear

skinny rib - mens/
womenswear

twin set -
womenswear

cardigan - mens/womenswear

tank top - mens/womenswear

Aran
sweater -
mens/
womens
wear

bra (wrap-over) - womenswear

flattener brassiere - womenswear

bosom amplifier - womenswear

bandalette - womenswear

strapless bra - womenswear

sports bra - womenswear

(back view)

balconette bra - womenswear

apodesme - womenswear

underwired bra - womenswear

Wonderbra™ uplift - womenswear

bustier - womenswear

fifties uplift - womenswear

gourgandine - womenswear

backless bra - womenswear

basque - womenswear

suspender belt - womenswear

longline bra - womenswear

(back view)

merry widow - womenswear

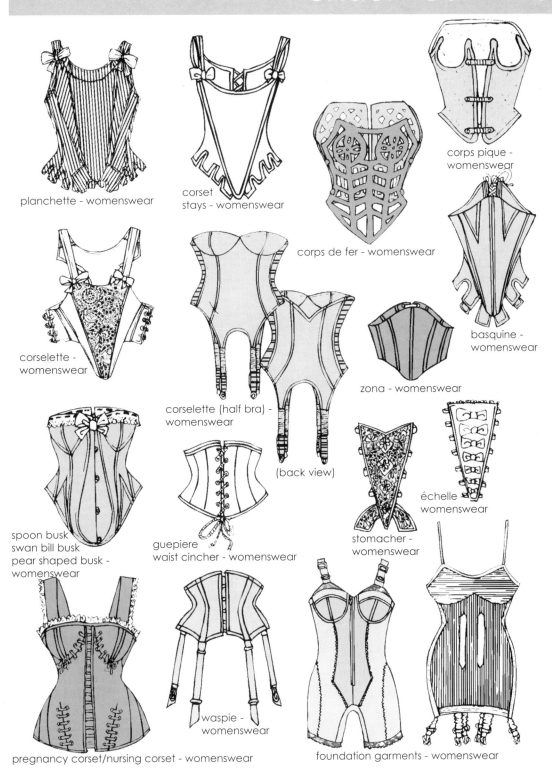

planchette - womenswear

corset
stays - womenswear

corps de fer - womenswear

corps pique -
womenswear

basquine -
womenswear

corselette -
womenswear

corselette (half bra) -
womenswear

(back view)

zona - womenswear

échelle
womenswear

spoon busk
swan bill busk
pear shaped busk -
womenswear

guepiere
waist cincher - womenswear

stomacher -
womenswear

pregnancy corset/nursing corset - womenswear

waspie -
womenswear

foundation garments - womenswear

vest - mens/womenswear

string vest - menswear

thermal vest - womenswear

girdle with suspenders - womenswear

leotard - womenswear

thong aerobics brief - womenswear

(back view)

bodyshaper - womenswear

teddy - womenswear

briefs - womenswear

G-string - womenswear

French knickers cami-knickers - womenswear

Y fronts - menswear

thermals - womenswear

combinaire - womenswear

loincloth - menswear

pantie girdle - womenswear

underdrawers - womenswear

peasant drawers - menswear

boxer shorts - menswear

knickerbocker bloomer - womenswear

drawstring drawers womenswear

umbrella drawers - womenswear

knickerbockers - womenswear

opera drawers - womenswear

French drawers - womenswear

dance set - womenswear

Directoire knickers - womenswear

brassiere - womenswear

camesia - womenswear

envelope chemise - womens wear

chemiset - womenswear

chemise slip - womens wear

combination corset cover and knickerbockers - womenswear

half slip - womenswear

gored petticoat with dust ruffles - womenswear

(side view)

bustle petticoat - womenswear

(side view)

bustle petticoat with button-on underskirt - womenswear

petticoat (boned) - womenswear

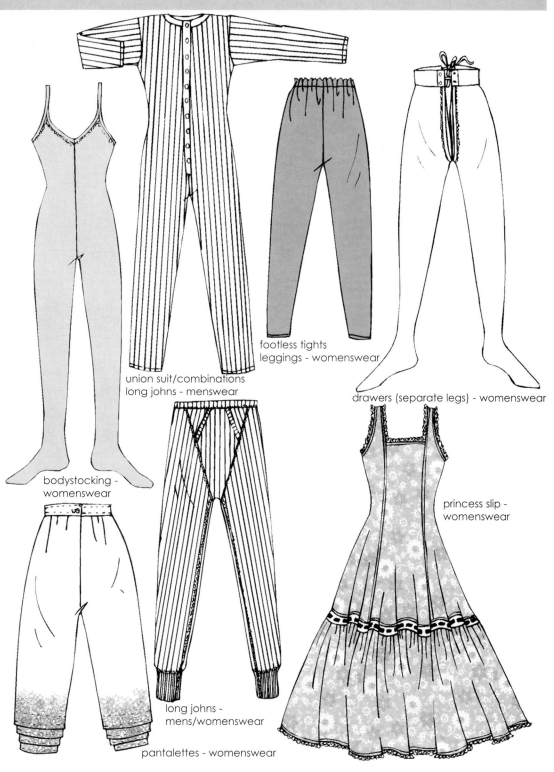

union suit/combinations
long johns - menswear

footless tights
leggings - womenswear

drawers (separate legs) - womenswear

bodystocking -
womenswear

princess slip -
womenswear

long johns -
mens/womenswear

pantalettes - womenswear

ski underwear - mens/womenswear

tobe - mens/womenswear

stola - womenswear

bustle (spiral wire) - womenswear

crinoline hoop (steel) - womenswear

plastic frame crinoline - womenswear

panniers (metal) - womenswear

pleated crinoline wheel - womenswear

farthingale bolster
waist bolster
bum barrel - womenswear

janseniste panniers - womenswear

bustle cushion - womenswear

sleeve cushions - womenswear

bustle crinoline - womenswear

criade - womenswear

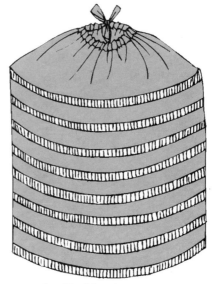

wheel farthingale - womenswear

clutch

pillow

envelope clutch

chain/Chanel

shoulder bag
top handle

swagger pouch

basket bag

bracelet handle

sausage

double bag
(central clasp)

(closed)

crescent shaped

almoner purse

evening bag

string bag

evening bag with
pantographic
fastening
(open)

feed

reticule

mesh evening
bag

document case

tote

bandoleer
pouch

Sally jess

Kelly

shoe bag

barrel bag

carpet bag

luggage handle

hat box

muff

box bag

vanity box

wig box

fishing bag

bucket

Oxford bag

duffle

ski bag

lifestyle bag

courier bag for cycle

rucksack

bum bag

roll holdall

panniers

sports bag

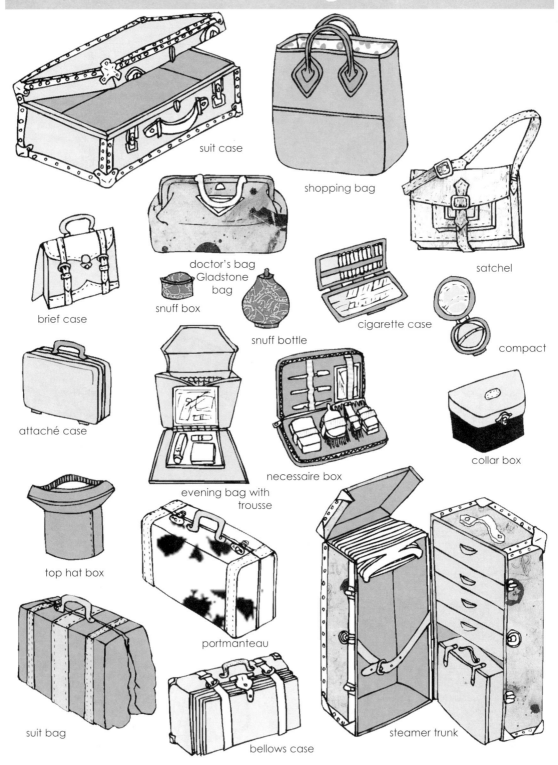

suit case

shopping bag

doctor's bag
Gladstone
bag

satchel

brief case

snuff box

snuff bottle

cigarette case

compact

attaché case

necessaire box

collar box

evening bag with
trousse

top hat box

portmanteau

steamer trunk

suit bag

bellows case

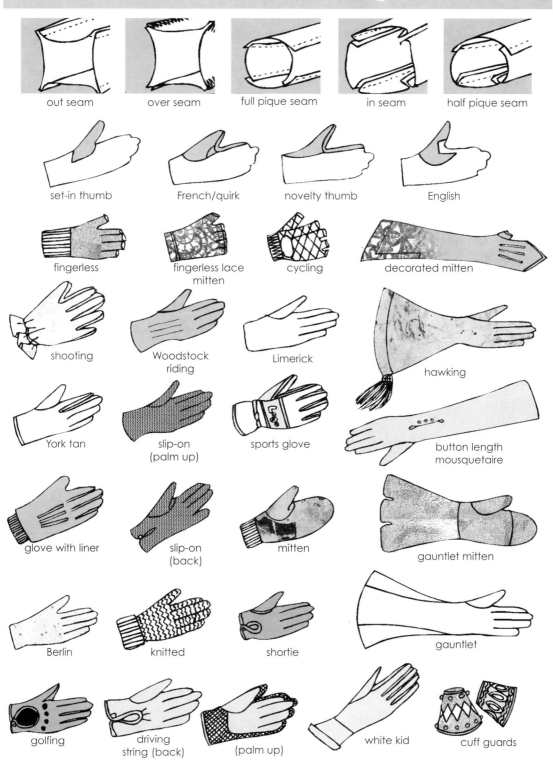

out seam   over seam   full pique seam   in seam   half pique seam

set-in thumb   French/quirk   novelty thumb   English

fingerless   fingerless lace mitten   cycling   decorated mitten

shooting   Woodstock riding   Limerick   hawking

York tan   slip-on (palm up)   sports glove   button length mousquetaire

glove with liner   slip-on (back)   mitten   gauntlet mitten

Berlin   knitted   shortie   gauntlet

golfing   driving string (back)   (palm up)   white kid   cuff guards

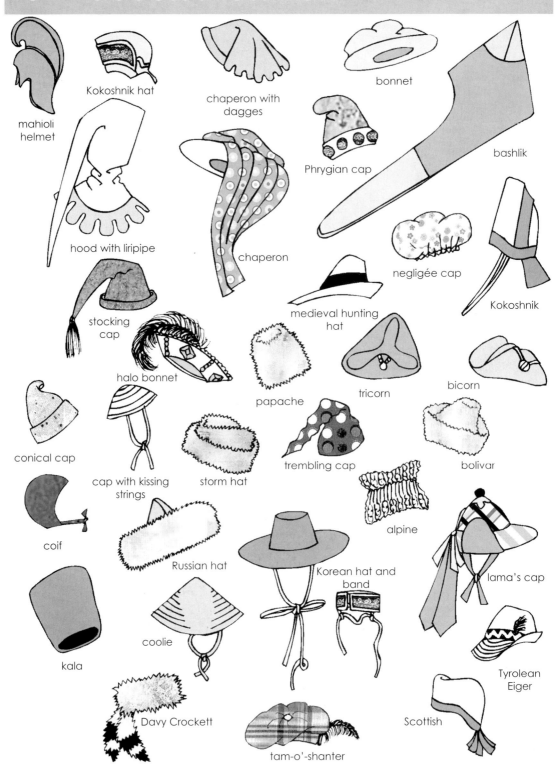

mahioli helmet

Kokoshnik hat

chaperon with dagges

bonnet

Phrygian cap

bashlik

hood with liripipe

chaperon

negligée cap

Kokoshnik

stocking cap

medieval hunting hat

halo bonnet

papache

tricorn

bicorn

conical cap

cap with kissing strings

storm hat

trembling cap

bolivar

coif

Russian hat

alpine

lama's cap

kala

coolie

Korean hat and band

Davy Crockett

tam-o'-shanter

Scottish

Tyrolean Eiger

trooper

G.I. helmet liner

cloth cap

Beatle cap

motoring cap

fez

pith helmet safari

field

bobble hat with pom pom

beret

plantation

Nehru service

muffin

French sailor cap

top hat

ten gallon with hat band

puggaree   hat band

bush hat

smoking cap

Breton

bowler Derby

stovepipe

Australian military

stetson

school cap

baseball cap

helmet with chin strap

sombrero barbiqueio (chin strap)

fedora

homburg

deerstalker

balaclava

bushman

pork pie

domed cricket

sou'wester

panama

trilby

ski mask

Gibson girl

gypsy straw

lampshade straw

bergere milkmaid

cartwheel

boater

picture

Gainsborough

gob's sailor

capeline skimmer

beehive bonnet

slouch

riding bowler

sailor pie plate

sun hat

riding hat

cloche

bucket

sugar loaf

half hat

pill box

Eugenie

hair bag

wimple

skull cap Juliet cap

Watteau with hat pin

taboosh

pagri

kaffiyeh with egal

headrail   couvrechief

litham

khat

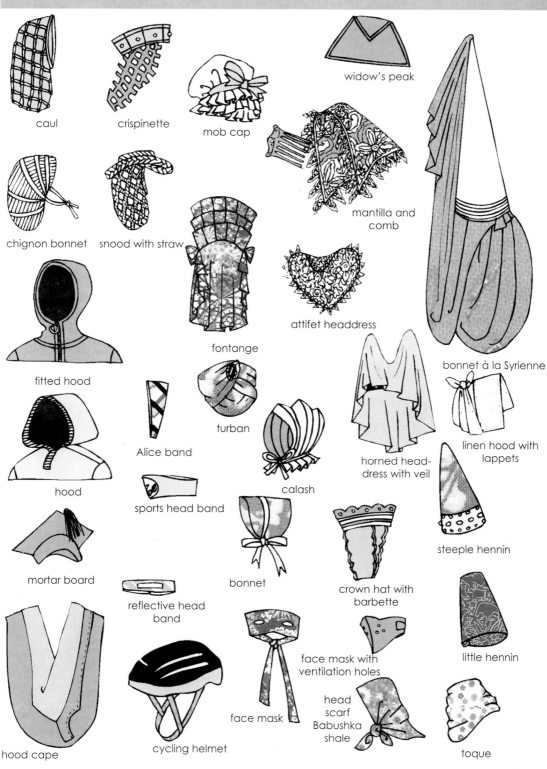

caul

crispinette

mob cap

widow's peak

chignon bonnet

snood with straw

mantilla and comb

attifet headdress

fitted hood

fontange

bonnet à la Syrienne

hood

turban

Alice band

horned head-dress with veil

linen hood with lappets

sports head band

calash

steeple hennin

mortar board

bonnet

reflective head band

crown hat with barbette

little hennin

hood cape

cycling helmet

face mask

face mask with ventilation holes

head scarf Babushka shale

toque

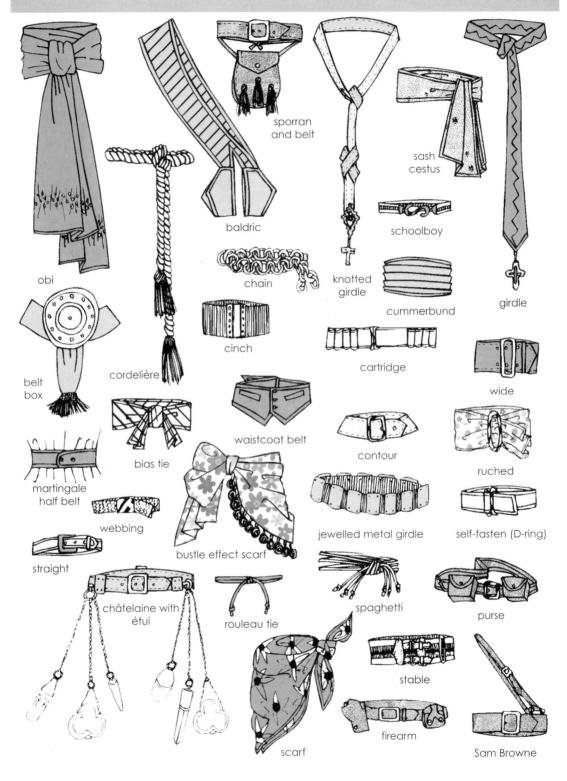

obi

baldric

sporran and belt

sash

cestus

schoolboy

chain

knotted girdle

cummerbund

girdle

belt box

cordelière

cinch

cartridge

wide

waistcoat belt

contour

ruched

martingale half belt

bias tie

jewelled metal girdle

self-fasten (D-ring)

webbing

straight

bustle effect scarf

châtelaine with étui

rouleau tie

spaghetti

purse

stable

scarf

firearm

Sam Browne

fichu

spotted handkerchief

Ascot

string tie

lariat tie with aiglet points

chemisette

Steinkirk

de Joinville

kipper tie

flat scarf

tie

dickie

Napolean tie Corsican

four-in-hand

Croatian

cravat with pin

muffler

1950s tie

cloud

neckerchief

bow tie

schoolboy scarf

stock

Yankee necktie

face muffler

stock (opened out)

military stock

incroyable cravat

feather boa

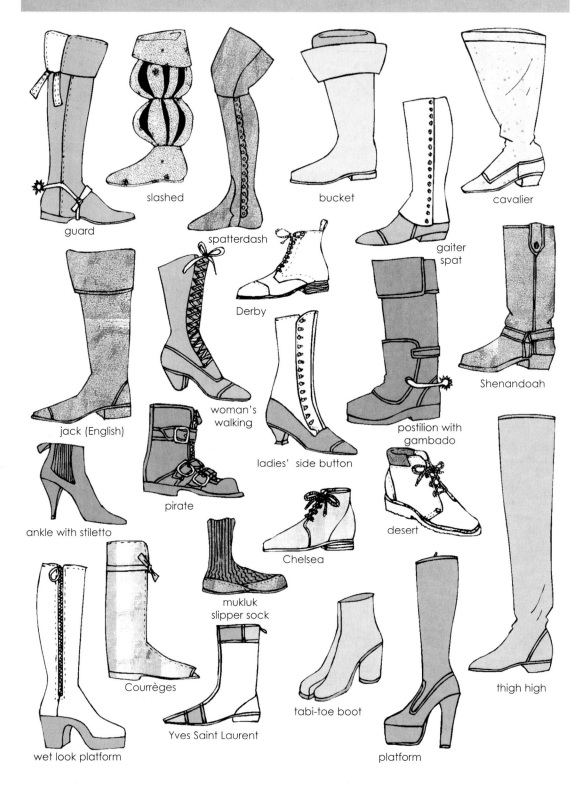

guard

slashed

spatterdash

bucket

cavalier

gaiter spat

Derby

woman's walking

jack (English)

pirate

ladies' side button

postilion with gambado

Shenandoah

ankle with stiletto

Chelsea

desert

mukluk slipper sock

Courrèges

wet look platform

Yves Saint Laurent

tabi-toe boot

platform

thigh high

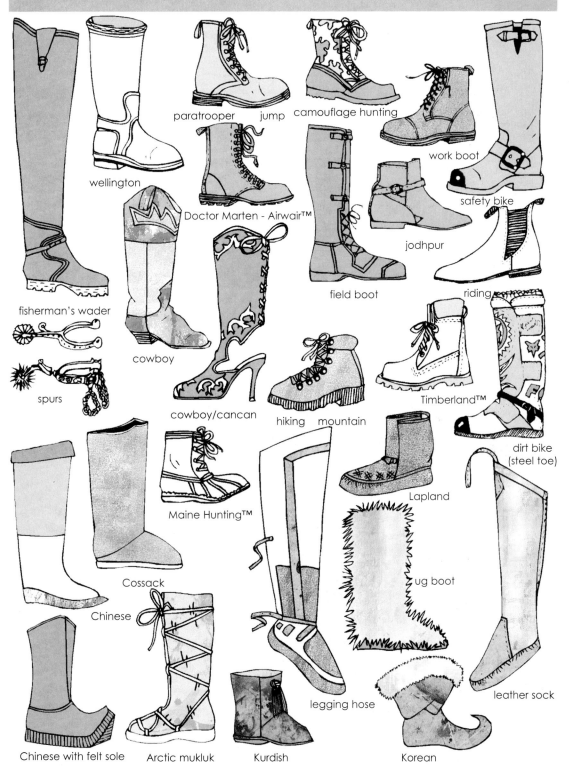

wellington

paratrooper

jump

camouflage hunting

work boot

safety bike

fisherman's wader

Doctor Marten - Airwair™

jodhpur

riding

spurs

cowboy

field boot

cowboy/cancan

hiking

mountain

Timberland™

dirt bike
(steel toe)

Maine Hunting™

Lapland

ug boot

Cossack

Chinese

legging hose

leather sock

Chinese with felt sole

Arctic mukluk

Kurdish

Korean

piked

high tongue

poulaine

Persian slipper

rose window

Moroccan slipper

cresida sandal

babouche slipper

caliga sandal

chopine

hobnailed and sole

knob style

Chinese shoe (bound feet)

pampootie

pantofle medieval overshoe

kub-kob

palm leaf sandal

moccasin

patten

sabot

baxea sandal

black jack

clog

galosh (men's)

Shetland clog

men's sandal

spat

galosh (women's)

blucher (US)

Jesus sandal

saddle

co-respondent

slip-on

Oxford

dress

Balmoral

loafer with tassels

brogue

winkle picker

brothel creeper
beetle crusher

Rockports™

dance

platform with sling-
back

no heel

peep-toe wedge
with sling-back

gymnastic

Louis heel

huarache

espadrille

ankle strap

stiletto heel

d'Orsay

court

mule

stacked heel

T-bar

Cuban heel

ballet pump

cloven toe

opera pump

invisible shoe

ghillie

V-throat

spectator

brass shoe

simple sandal

Canadian
snowshoe

Mary Jane

flip flop

Japanese snowshoe

hi-top trainer

American football

aerobic

football lineman (US)

training

cycling shoe cover

bicycling with sole

boat deck

retro trainer

weight lifting

boxing

baseball Converse Allstars™

peep-toe trainer

distressed trainer

side-fastening trainer

neoprene™ trainer

roller blade effect

platform trainer

strap-fastening trainer

trainer mule

backless Allstars™

après sport sandal

golf shoe

soccer boot

high heeled sneaker

platform trainer exaggerated

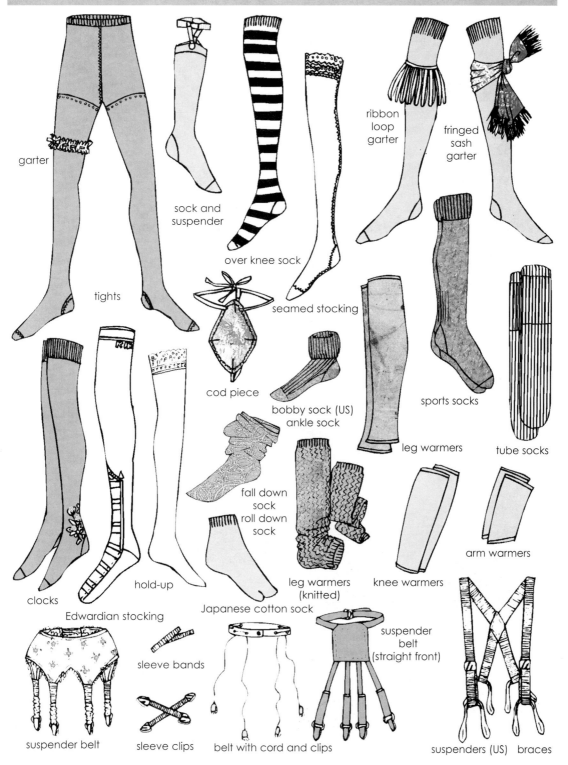

garter

sock and suspender

over knee sock

ribbon loop garter

fringed sash garter

tights

seamed stocking

cod piece

bobby sock (US) ankle sock

sports socks

leg warmers

tube socks

clocks

hold-up

Edwardian stocking

fall down sock roll down sock

Japanese cotton sock

leg warmers (knitted)

knee warmers

arm warmers

suspender belt

sleeve bands

sleeve clips

belt with cord and clips

suspender belt (straight front)

suspenders (US) braces

flatlock seam

zig-zagged seam

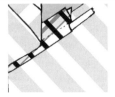

piping

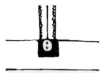

weighted hem
with lead discs

superlock seam

stitched and
pinked seam

binding

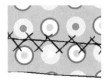

herringbone stitch

flatlock and over-
locked together

run and fell seam

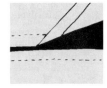

slot seam

hem (mitred
corner)

exposed seam

mock run and fell
seam

faggoting

weighted hem
with lead pellets

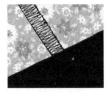

Rimoldi

fur seam

boning/stay strip

weighted hem with
chain - Chanel style

French seam

lace seam

taped seam

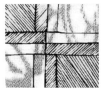

intersecting/crossed seam

couching

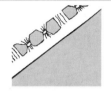

drawn thread work

blanket stitch

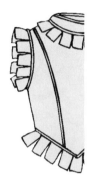

piccadills

gusset

trapunto

flounce

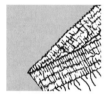

elastic webbing

handmade eyelet

wadded quilting

gallant

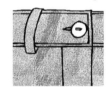

belt loops/carriers

slashing

fringing

knitted rib

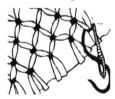

smocking
(honeycomb stitch

dagges

casing with drawstring

pleated frill

machine embroidery

dagges

fitchet

turn-up

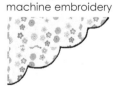

scalloped edge

picot edge

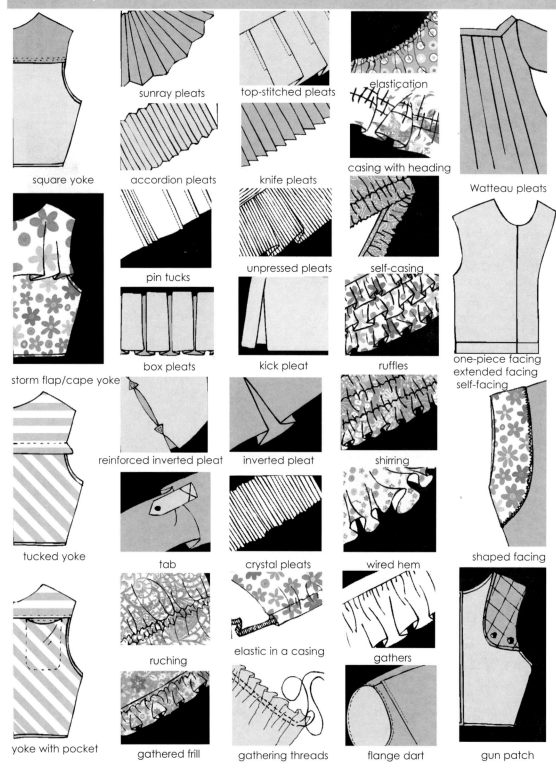

sunray pleats

top-stitched pleats

elastication

casing with heading

square yoke

accordion pleats

knife pleats

Watteau pleats

pin tucks

unpressed pleats

self-casing

storm flap/cape yoke

box pleats

kick pleat

ruffles

one-piece facing
extended facing
self-facing

reinforced inverted pleat

inverted pleat

shirring

tucked yoke

tab

crystal pleats

wired hem

shaped facing

yoke with pocket

ruching

elastic in a casing

gathers

gathered frill

gathering threads

flange dart

gun patch

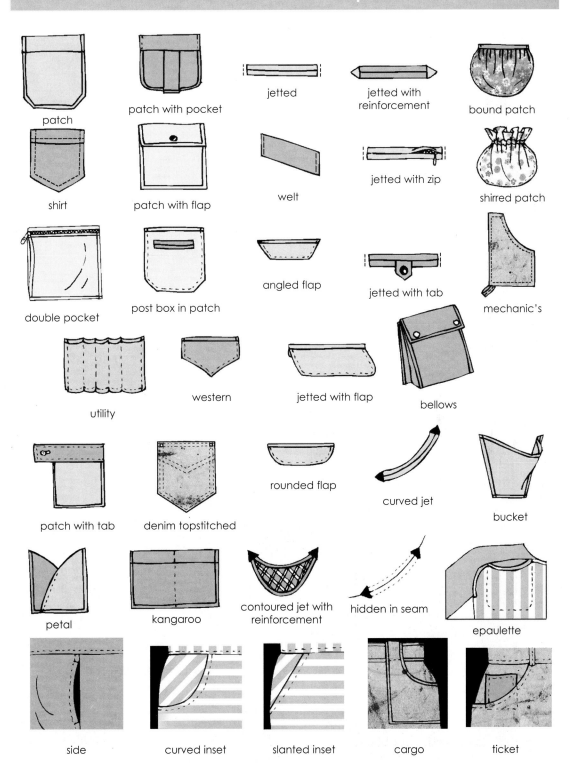

patch

patch with pocket

jetted

jetted with reinforcement

bound patch

shirt

patch with flap

welt

jetted with zip

shirred patch

double pocket

post box in patch

angled flap

jetted with tab

mechanic's

utility

western

jetted with flap

bellows

patch with tab

denim topstitched

rounded flap

curved jet

bucket

petal

kangaroo

contoured jet with reinforcement

hidden in seam

epaulette

side

curved inset

slanted inset

cargo

ticket

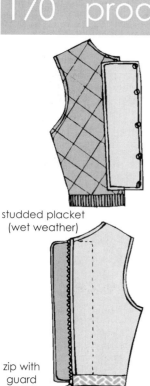

studded placket
(wet weather)

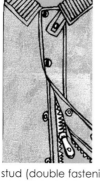

zip with
guard

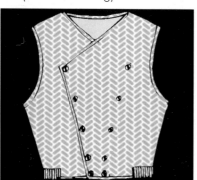

zip and stud (double fastening)

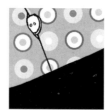

asymmetrical fastening

four- and two-hole
sew-through button

woman's fastening

man's fastening

self-shank button

metal shank

hook and eye

toggle fastening

reinforced button

rouleau loops

covered button

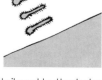

fur tack

in-seam
buttonhole

frog fastening

ratchet spring and
hook

tailored buttonholes

popper/press stud
snap fastening (US)

snap tape

Velcro™

hook and eye
fastening

gimp covered fur
hook and eye

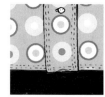

button placket
(topstitched)

dog clip

reversible zip

cord loop

brace clip
suspender clip

hook and bar

hook and eye
(strip)

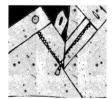

thread loop

bra hook
swimsuit hook

overall adjuster
and buckle

anchor buckle

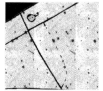

commercial braid
soutache

D-rings

interlocking fastener

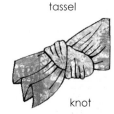

tassel

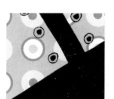

man's fly front with
French bearer

buckles

tie fastening

knot

fly front (closed)

metal eyelet

lacing

bow

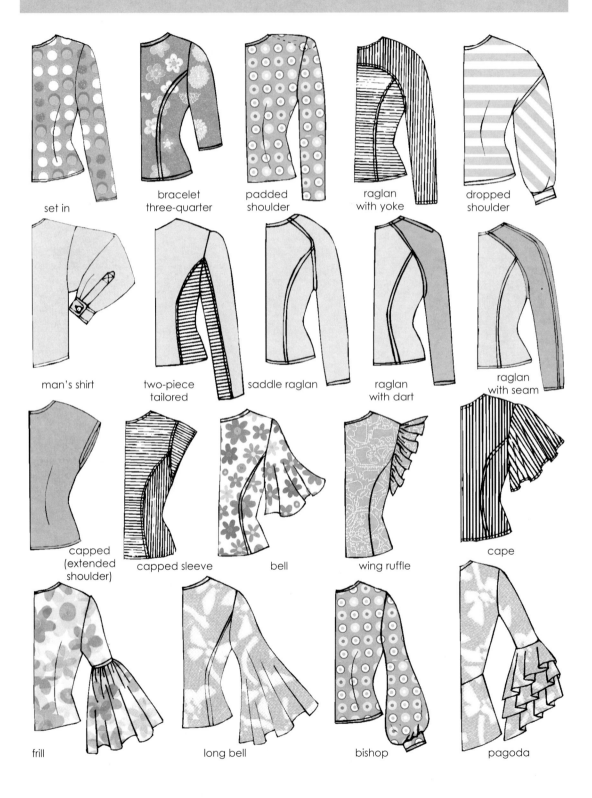

set in

bracelet
three-quarter

padded
shoulder

raglan
with yoke

dropped
shoulder

man's shirt

two-piece
tailored

saddle raglan

raglan
with dart

raglan
with seam

capped
(extended
shoulder)

capped sleeve

bell

wing ruffle

cape

frill

long bell

bishop

pagoda

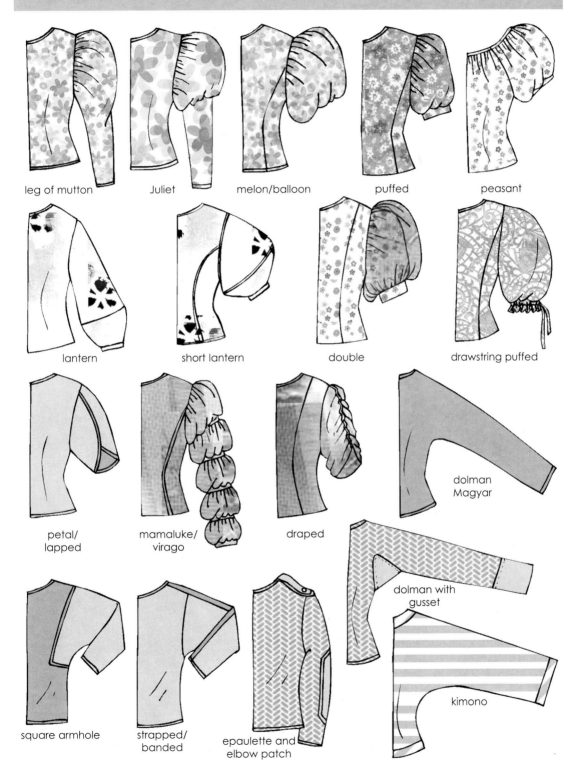

leg of mutton

Juliet

melon/balloon

puffed

peasant

lantern

short lantern

double

drawstring puffed

petal/
lapped

mamaluke/
virago

draped

dolman
Magyar

dolman with
gusset

square armhole

strapped/
banded

epaulette and
elbow patch

kimono

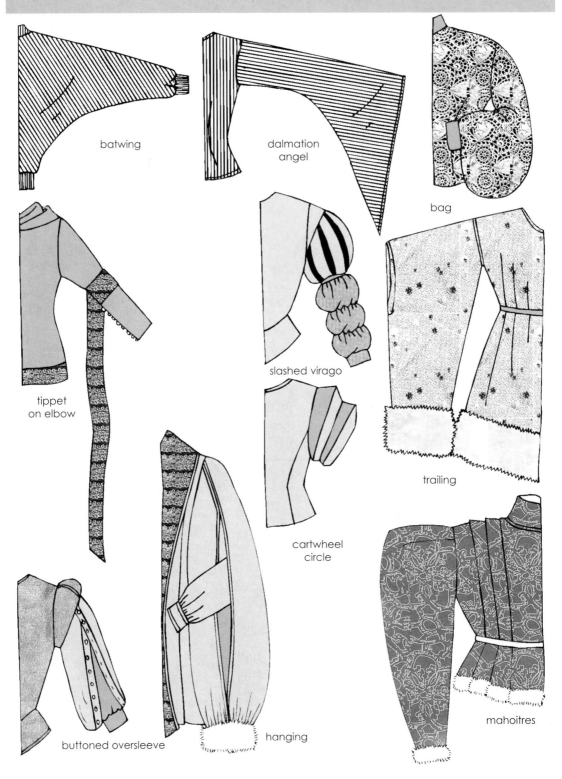

batwing

dalmation angel

bag

tippet on elbow

slashed virago

trailing

cartwheel circle

buttoned oversleeve

hanging

mahoitres

faced hem shaped faced hem faced placket man's tailored shirt loose pleat cuff angled

curved turn back turn-up French with cuff links long fitted button tab

gauntlet western tramline/ top-stitched rouleau loop button vent

button extension zipped bound wedge inset fringed elasticated cuff

buckle and strap elasticated with frill ruched placket with gathers drawstring ribbed knitted

straight band

bateau

ring

polo
turtle
roll

mandarin   Nehru

Peter Pan

asymmetrical straight band

Cossack

bishop

tab

convertible closed

convertible open

shirt collar with stand tailored

button down

giraffe

Danton

wing tipped

shawl

Napolean high coat/high-
wayman/
high
fold

revers

clover revers

tuxedo

fishmouth revers

shaped shawl

Italian

L-revers

Chelsea

portrait

sailor (front)

sailor (back)

puritan

round Bertha

square Bertha

Dutch

Pierrot

ruff

falling band

vandyke

gorget

partlet

standing band

barbette

carcaille

cascade jabot

modesty piece

Ascot

bow tie

central stitched ruffle

bib with frill

tuxedo

Eton

Betsie

canezou

collarette with décolleté

basic plain jewel

U-neckline

scoop

square

horseshoe

built-up/funnel

sweetheart

décolleté

wide square

V-neckline

halter

bateau

slashed

sabrina

one shoulder

keyhole

scalloped

inset

envelope

crew

wrap-over bateau

racing   athletic
(back)

strapless (princess line)

off the shoulder

high cowl

mitred neck

cowl inset

elasticised

drawstring

wide cowl

graduated ruffle

sugar bag

ruffle set-in seam

pleated ruffle

circular ruffle

empire line

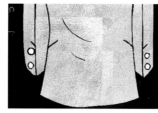

no vent

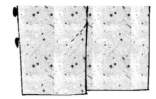

vented hem

dropped waist

single vent

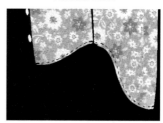

basic curved shirt

high waist

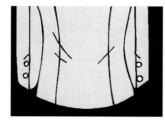

double vent

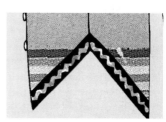

poncho trimmed

bandless and faced

peplum

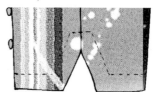

V-notched and faced

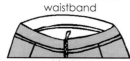

waistband

paper bag

dropped back

hipster

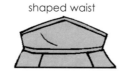

shaped waist

wrap-over

nightshirt

yoke

shaped waistband

drawstring

CHILDREN'S PROPORTIONS

The following information is meant as an average guide to the capabilities of children at certain ages. In reality progress depends upon the individual child, but it is still useful to know the developmental stages.

The guidance about proportion is always given in HEAD LENGTHS. This is a common tool and includes the head in any example given. Regardless of the actual height in metric or imperial measurement, the proportion, by using the length of the head, does work to help plan a drawing.

Many of the children's figures provided show clothing, this is kept as simple as possible to indicate where seam lines are, how garments drape and fall on children and how they wear hats, shoes and other accessories.

All of this information is essential to communicate convincingly a clothing design for a child.

Newborn 0–3 months   Page 1

The head is large in proportion to the body, the newborn being approximately three and a half to four heads in length. The arms and legs are very small, the nose is very short and it is typical to see the newborn with its hands forming a fist. The first smile appears around six weeks of age.

3–9 months   Page 2–3

Babies are approximately four heads in length and have a very rounded appearance. The baby starts to sit up around six months and takes an interest in its surroundings. The baby then becomes more active and begins crawling.

10–12 months   Page 4

Babies are approximately four heads in height and are still very rounded with protruding tummies. Some babies are pulling themselves up on furniture and are taking their first faltering steps.

12–14 months   Page 5

The proportions are still roughly four heads in height. The baby is gaining more confidence in its walking and could now be referred to as a toddler. The toddler is beginning to say a few words. The toddler's body weight triples and the height doubles in the first year after birth.

14–20 months   Page 6

The proportions are still four heads in height. The toddler is developing both in its speech and in movement. The toddler is beginning to feed itself with a spoon – very messy!

20–24 months   Page 7

The proportions are still unchanged, but the child is becoming more dextrous and adding more words to its speech, forming simple sentences.

2–2½ years   Page 8

The child is building on its speech and movement, but the proportions remain unchanged.

2½–4 years   Page 9–10

The proportions are beginning to change from four heads to four and a half approximately in height. At around the age of three years the limbs become longer and co-ordination is improved. At around the age of four years the child has a full set of twenty milk teeth and also starts nursery school.

5–6 years   Page 11–12

The proportions are roughly four and a half heads in height, the child is beginning to lose its baby fat, the legs are becoming longer and thinner, the front teeth start to fall out from six years of age.

7–9 years   Pages 13–15

The proportions are approximately five heads in height. The rate of growth of the bones slows down around the age of seven to ten years. The adult teeth start to appear as molars. At seven years of age the brain begins to produce sex hormones and these increase in concentration over the next few years. This is a period when the activities of boys and girls alter and separate.

10–11 years   Page 16–17

There are roughly five and a half heads to the height of the child. The rate of growth of bones starts to speed up again just before puberty. The child appears to be leggy and awkward.

12–14 years   Pages 18–21

The child's proportions are now roughly six heads in height and this age group should more properly be termed teenagers. Different children start puberty at different ages, depending on the quality of their diet. At puberty the sex organs mature and secondary changes occur, that is, a girl will develop breasts and a boy's voice will break.

NB: Do not change the proportions of the child to fit in with the adult approach to the fashion figure, this will distort the child's body and change its apparent age.

MEN'S AND WOMEN'S PROPORTIONS
PAGES 22–49

After puberty the body matures into full adulthood. Muscular strength is built up and the long bones stop growing. A man is at his muscular and sexual peak between the ages of eighteen and twenty-five years and a woman is at her most fertile at the age of twenty-eight years. The height is seven and a half heads.

The figures provided are from almost 'real life'. No excessive lengthening of the body or legs is evident. The lengthening of the figure depends on the 'fashion' in fashion illustration. For example, in the 1960s legs were very long in proportion to the rest of the body. Fashion proportions, recently, are more realistic at around eight head lengths.

The following recommendations are for use as a guide only, dependent on how the figures are developed.

Women's figures   Pages 22–25
This figure has a modern, sporty 'look'. She would be useful when designing for the middle market, high street and cult orientated street fashion.

Women's figures   Page 26–29
This figure is of a young girl and would be particularly useful when designing for the teenage market.

Women's figures   Pages 30–33
This figure is quite feminine and would be useful when designing for the middle market and for high street fashion.

Women's figures   Page 34–37
This figure is quite sophisticated in its fashion poses and would be useful at a high fashion level. The figure could also be developed for use in swimwear and underwear illustration.

Men's figures   Pages 38–41
This figure would be useful for young, possibly slightly androgynous design work. Particularly at middle market and the cult orientated street level of the market.

Men's figures   Pages 42–45
A solid, clean cut, sporty looking figure, good for fashion at all levels of the market except the cult orientated street level.

Men's figures   Pages 46–49
A figure that is useful at many levels of the market with a little development, quite strong and sporty. Useful for high fashion to high street.

Adult proportions tend to be approximately seven and a half heads in height (including the head). The length of the body from the top of the neck to the crutch is about three heads in length. The legs are about three and a half heads in length from the top of the leg to the sole of the foot. Hips are approximately one and a half heads in width. The upper part of the arm is approximately one head in length. The foot is slightly longer than the length of the head.

The head itself can be broken down into proportions to help in successful fashion drawing. The eyeline is halfway down the total length of the head. The bottom of the nose rests halfway between the eyeline and the chin and the mouth is halfway between the chin and the base of the nose. The ear lies in a parallel to the nose, this is more obvious when the head is viewed in profile. In this position the head looks a lot wider.

There is no substitute for observing and recording as accurately as possible when drawing.

FASHION ILLUSTRATION (FIGURE)

The first part of this book deals with figure proportion for use in fashion illustration.

A fashion illustration is used in the fashion industry to show information in a number of areas:

1. A mood or feeling that is relevant to current fashion.
2. To show a 'total look' including the styling of the pose, face, hair, hands and feet as well as the garment design.
3. The proportion and use of colour within an outfit/ garment.
4. The proportion and use of fabric combinations.
5. The proportion of detail in comparison to other garments in the outfit.
6. The balance of a collection of garments on a number of figures.

Fashion illustration on the figures is used widely in the industry, by fashion prediction companies, by designers, by large fashion companies creating ranges, by fashion magazines and trade journals, and by students.

The figures provided can be used as they are for fashion illustration or, can be subtly extended/exaggerated to over eight heads in height for a more extreme fashion feeling. Extra length can be added at the waist, through the thighs and through the calf. The approach for men's and women's figures is the same.

Do not change the length of the children's figures as this will distort the figure and change the apparent age of the child. When different approaches to fashion drawing are adopted, i.e. stylised/cartoon effect figures, then proportion may appear distorted but the desired effect is still achieved. A successful result depends upon the final uses of the fashion illustration.

TECHNICAL/FLAT/WORKING AND SPECIFICATION DRAWING

The second part of this book shows a number of drawings of garments for men, women and children. It is hoped that they will provide a starting point for design projects in any fashion area or market level. This section was designed to cover as much as possible about clothing, garment construction, garment finishes and accessories as was physically possible within the confines of the book. The device used to illustrate these points was the technical, flat or working drawing. The specification or 'spec' drawing is principally the same but with the addition of specifications such as measurements – details on proportion for manufacturer, information about trims, fabrication, colour etc. The other types of drawing can also include this type of information but do not always do so.

Technical/flat/working and specification drawing is used for a number of reasons:

1. To show accurate proportion.
2. To show construction lines/seams.
3. To show detail and positioning of detail including fastenings, trims and finishes.
4. To aid in building garment ranges.
5. To report from trade fairs.
6. To illustrate comparative and directional shop reports.
7. To supplement a fashion/figure illustration – indicating detail obscured by layers of garments and back views.

This type of drawing is used in every area of the fashion industry. It is used in fashion prediction to show design, trade fair reports, shop reports, sampling of garments. It is used in manufacturing by designers, pattern cutters, and sample machinists. It is used in range building and presentations. It is also a very important first step in the training of a fashion student.

The wide range of uses of a technical drawing make it essential that the drawing is always clear and precise in its rendering. There should be no detail open to misinterpretation.

WOMAN
8 heads page 22

MAN
8 heads page 42

CHILD 14–20 MONTHS
4 heads page 6

FIGURE 1

FIGURE 2

FIGURE 3

FIGURE 4

FIGURE 5

A perpendicular can be dropped through the centre of the head to the ground. If the model is posing with weight equally on both feet then the perpendicular will be central to the legs (see child's pose FIGURE 3). If there is weight on one foot only then the perpendicular will pass through the centre of this foot. This acts as a guide to balancing the figure realistically on the page.

Extra length may be added to the figure to increase the height for fashion purposes. Here, the increase is by about three-quarters of a head, thus making the finished figure height as approximately eight and three-quarter heads. The extra length is added through the waist and arms together – A, the thigh – B and calf – C, FIGURES 4 and 5.

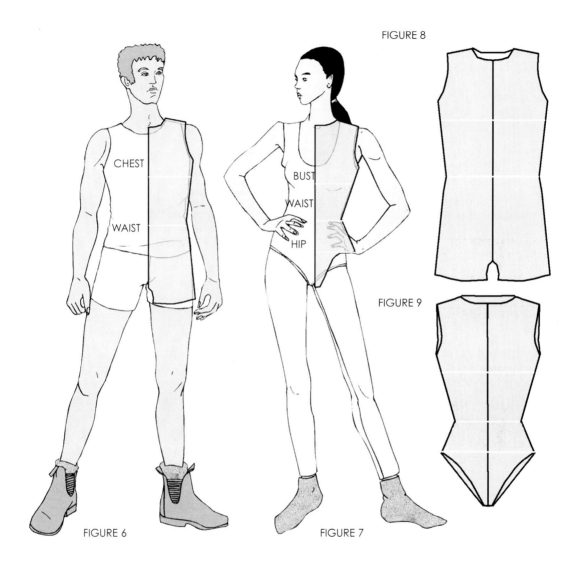

FIGURE 8

FIGURE 9

FIGURE 6

FIGURE 7

FIGURES 6 and 7 show how to develop a body template for technical, flat, working or specification drawings. The CENTRE line of the body is defined, then the body shape is traced on one side only to produce an appropriate template for mens or womenswear.

The template is then 'mirrored' for a full body shape – FIGURES 8 and 9. The CENTRE FRONT is always indicated (for guidance) as should be the WAIST, HIP and BUST/CHEST LINE, if appropriate.

These templates can be further developed by using the bodysuit as a base for developing other templates such as shirts, jackets and coats – each getting slightly larger as real garments would.

Back views of templates can be created by filling in the back neck, arm and leg holes of the bodysuit and then tracing off the new shape.

CHILDRENSWEAR
Page 50

Knitted Bootee: Not used so much these days with the advent of the stretch body suit, the bootee used to be essential on winter nights when worn with nightdresses. Babies are not good at maintaining body temperature and consequently they can become very cold or very hot quite quickly.

Slipper: Designed in many fabrics and worn with pyjamas, these slippers have a reinforced toe for rough and tough wear.

Padder: A soft bootee shape made in a variety of fabrics, worn by babies who are not yet walking.

Liberty Cap/Fisher Cap: A knitted cap in scarlet wool, reminiscent of the French revolutionaries 'liberty cap'.

Scratch Mits: Soft fabric mittens very simply shaped with ties, worn to prevent small babies scratching themselves.

Crossover Fichu with Sash: Popular fashion around the 1870s.

Moccasin: From the North American Indian, the Iroquois, made from suede with blue and orange raffia decoration. The sole and upper are made in the same fabric.

Roman Sandal: Leather shoe with multi-strap and button fastening, inspired by the high-backed Roman sandal.

Jelly Bean Sandal: Plastic moulded sandal in a variety of colours, may be transparent, opaque or even with a glitter finish.

Jesus Sandal: Sole held on the foot by two sets of straps, one wrapping around the ankle, usually made of leather.

Canvas Shoe: Sporty lace-up shoe with rubber sole.

Deck Shoe: This canvas shoe has an elastic inset in the upper. Elastic was invented in 1836 by Charles Goodyear and was used originally in shoes and garters. Elastic inserts at the side of shoes are also popular so that the shoes can be slipped on easily and maintain a good fit.

Mittens: Four fingers are covered together, the thumb is separate. This example is knitted with a decorative stripe and has a very useful string or tie attached for the mittens to be threaded through a coat or jacket so that they are not easily lost.

Suspenders (US)/Braces: Elasticated adjustable braces with clips for versatility, very useful when wearing trousers or leggings as the small child has no waist.

Argyle Sock: Inspired by the original plaid stockings of the Scottish Highlands, these are still a popular accessory today.

Bandanna: Red bandannas were a popular sight in America, worn by boys in all classes. They were also known as 'wipes' for mopping up perspiration.

Wellington: Waterproof boot worn originally by the Duke of Wellington. Here the boot is moulded to appeal to children and many designs are available.

Baseball Boot: Lace-up sport boot made of canvas with rubber sole and toe.

Training Shoe/Trainer: Very popular sports shoe, often with decorative and bright stripings applied to a wide base and often designed with Velcro™ fastenings.

Sailor Hat: Modelled from the adult hat and designed to go with the sailor suits that have been, and still are, popular fashion for boys and girls alike.

Sun Hat: Fabric hat, often a twill weave, with a wide brim to protect small children from the sun.

Sou'wester: Oilskin hat worn by fishermen and adopted by children because of the protection afforded by the sloping back covering the neck against stormy weather. Traditionally yellow in colour for visibility during storms.

Knitted Helmet: Worn by boys and girls for warmth with ear flaps and straps for snugness.

Ankle Sock: Short socks appeared in the 1840s in artists' portraits. They are universally worn today and come in a variety of colours and designs to co-ordinate with outfits or to reflect the trend in children's film heroes.

Tights: Knitted very finely or very chunkily or anything between, they come in a variety of stitches, colours and patterns for wear all year round by girls.

Knitted Hat: This particular hat is part of a set belonging to the mittens, often co-ordinated.

Glengarry Cap (US): A plaid cap with decorative ribbon usually worn with a short black jacket and plaid trousers and linen collar around 1840.

Cottage Style Bonnet: Worn from around the 1830s, usually being decorated with ribbons and sometimes feathers.

Shako Cap (US)/Yacht Cap: Popular in America worn mostly by boys but occasionally by girls, it became known as the yacht cap and was worn for sporting activities.

It has a stiff band all the way round the head and a patent leather visor.

Pudding Cap (two versions): The cap is padded to provide protection for the toddler should he or she fall and is made from a variety of fabrics.

Mob Hat/Sun Hat: Fitted loosely on the head, usually elasticated for small babies, made of cambric or muslin with a puffed caul and frilly border, and used for protection from the sun.

Beret: A circular piece of cloth, drawn together, here, with a knitted cuff.

Shaped Apron/Sash: Generally worn around 1885–1890, the fishwife effect (see **fishwife draped overskirt**) worn previously is no longer achieved by lifting the overskirt, but by the shaped sash or apron cut to the slight point at the front and gathered up at the back.

Page 51

Vest With Poppers (Newborn): Full length vest with poppers between the legs for easy access when changing the baby. The vest is quite shapeless to accommodate nappies.

All-in-one Vest: This vest also has poppers but between the legs, again for easy nappy changing, but it now also has an envelope neckline for comfort and ease of dressing a wriggling baby.

Bodysuit: Very similar to the vest, worn by small girls, but the fabric and colours vary now as the suit is worn as a tee shirt (also popular with adult women) the poppers between the legs make it easy to change the child. The full bodysuit is comfortable as it does not 'ride up' with wear.

Liberty Bodice: Popular in the 1920s and 1930s and up to the clothing shortages of the Second World War when mothers made their own, the liberty bodice gradually fell in popularity and was discontinued in 1974. The bodice was made from fleecy backed jersey with tape as a reinforcement.

Corded Stays: Generally made from cotton the stays were worn by both sexes for their first few years, in the mid nineteenth century. Boys stopped wearing them when they put on their first suit. Girls continued to wear longer and stiffer versions until they graduated to boned corsets.

Vest: This vest is normal body length and has an envelope neckline. It is worn at any age but is particularly useful when potty training and in the young child.

Bib: Made of towelling on the front and generally having a plastic or waterproof backing, the bib is used for soaking up liquids and foods when worn by the young child.

Babygro™/Stretch Coverall: Developed in the 1950s in America by Walter Artzt, he invented a number of fabrics and produced a new stretch fabric which he used in his design for a coverall for babies. The suit has feet and cuffs which can become mittens and also has poppers between the legs for ease in changing nappies – the epitome of comfort.

Night Drawers/Night Suit/Sleeper: Night drawers had sewn in feet and drop seats for the toddler's comfort. They were popular in the early 1900s and were made of merino wool or unbleached flannel.

Plastic Pants: Used to cover the terry towelling nappy and protect clothing from wetness, less popular these days because of the advent of the disposable nappy and its built-in plastic covering. Baby nappies were tied around the body until the twentieth century, even though the modern safety pin was designed and manufactured in the mid 1800s. The pin gradually took over, but, like the terry nappy, was usurped by the modern disposable nappy with its sticky fasteners. The trend is now, however, reversing with concern for environmental issues.

Pants/Briefs: Simple briefs, for small boys, without a fly.

Swimsuit: Girl's all-in-one swimsuit, very simple design, can also be decorated with frills and skirts.

Petticoat: Underskirt in cotton with simple trims, stops dresses from clinging to underwear and also adds an extra layer for warmth.

Bib with Sleeves: Same principle as an ordinary bib with towelling front and plastic back, the sleeves are also towelling and act as protection for clothing when the child is learning to feed itself.

Underskirt: Multi-layered underskirt to add shape to full dresses for special occasions.

Apron Bib (Side View): Plastic bib, totally waterproof and easy to wipe clean.

Page 52

Swaddling Set with Sleeves: Well into the eighteenth century babies were still dressed in the ancient method of swaddling. This consisted of binding the child tightly with bands of cloth, preventing it from moving in any direction. This was due to a belief that it would protect the child from falls and accidents as well as encouraging the straightness of legs and arms. The practice did, in fact, inhibit healthy growth. In the eighteenth century young babies, in the upper classes at least, were unbound at about six weeks old and simply dressed in the long clothes previously placed on top of the swaddling bands. Long clothes consisted of a short-sleeved gown about three feet (1 m) long and a cap decorated with lace and embroidery – see **christening robe**.

Swaddling Shirt: This was placed under the bindings and has gussets set in under the arms. There are drawstrings at the cuff.

Buster Suit: A small boy's buster suit hand knitted in rayon from the early 1930s.

Tee Shirt: Classic pull on top of cult status worn by adults and children alike, the tee shirt knows no social boundaries. Generally made in jersey with a rib knitted crew neckline, it developed from underwear. It may be decorated in a multitude of prints, patterns, motifs and colours. This child's example has a button fastening on one shoulder to allow fit over the head.

Knitted Pram Set: In the 1880s Dr Gustav Jaeger developed the Sanitary Woollen System – applying health principles to clothing. A Mr LRS Tomalin brought the system to Britain in 1884 and acquired British rights in the Jaeger name, consequently, selling Jaeger clothing. The apparent health giving properties of wool made it immediately fashionable and children were among the first to benefit. For generations to come wool next the skin was rule for all mothers. This is an example of a knitted suit from the 1920s.

Baby Romper: A one-piece suit, but giving the effect of shorts and top, from 1915 to 1920, made in silk with embroidery.

Swaddling Clothes and Bonnet: See above – **swaddling set with sleeves**.

North American Indian Shirt: Decorative shirt in a simple trapeze cut with gussets under each arm to aid in 'lift'.

Romper Suit: Designed to crawl in, with access between the legs for easy changing, this example has smocking detail.

Skirt Brief: One piece garment that is useful in the summer for covering nappies but still allowing the toddler to be cool by baring her legs.

Pyjamas: These pyjamas have a gusset between the legs for ease of movement and a co-ordinating top with collar. This style is generally made in a knitted jersey.

Page 53

Leggings: Elasticated body-hugging trouser, generally made in knitted jersey to give some stretch, can be printed or plain.

Baby Jeans: Denim jeans with all the details of an adult pair of jeans, plus an elasticated waist for pulling on as well as the fly fastener. The jeans also have button-through legs for easy nappy changing (see **denim jeans** (the adult version) for full description on origin).

Jumper (US)/Pinafore (Two Versions): This is a modern version of a pinafore. It has tie fastens and is derived from dungaree styling but manufactured in a pretty print. This second version of a pinafore has a finely pleated trim and tie waist, it could be worn with Roman sandals.

Dungaree Dress: Derived from the original dungaree – the workman's bibbed overall with adjustable straps – and re-interpreted for small girls, (see adult **dungarees** for a fuller description).

Kilt: Skirt of the Scottish Highlanders, made in tartan plaid with knife pleats and self fringe, it was adopted as childrenswear with the addition of adjustable crossover straps for the very small child (due to their non-existent waists).

All-Over Apron: A full-flared garment with long sleeves and collar, meant as protection for day clothes and worn by children aged two to six years. A belt is sewn into the side seams and fastens at the back. There is always a pocket on the front of the garment.

Apron with Betsie Collar: A simple dress and apron that was worn straight or draped in some way. The draping was purely aesthetic, but at least it meant that the child had one less skirt to worry about. The apron and dress were worn with a 'Betsie' collar derived from the ruff worn by Elizabeth I.

Drill Dress/Gymslip: The gymslip was seen as a revolutionary item when it emerged in the early 1900s. It was worn with matching regulation knickers with elastication at the knees and generally made in wool. By the 1920s the gymslip became compulsory in many private, convent and high schools but not at elementary schools.

Pinafore and Guimpe: The American term for the pinafore is the jumper, worn over the guimpe or blouse. This late nineteenth century pinafore had round, V-shaped, square, heart-shaped or high necks. Circular sleeves were the most popular, but puffed and long sleeves were also seen. The bodice was full and long and bloused in the front, this example was worn with a self-belt, the skirt was pleated and gathered and cut with a wide flare. The guimpe usually had three-quarter sleeves with cuffs or flounces at the elbow and they were decorated with rows of inserted lace and tucks.

Page 54

Jumpsuit: Empire line jumpsuit with side fastenings and puffed sleeves, it is trimmed with lace and worn by a very young child.

Brownie Suit (US)/Overalls: An American term for a play overall/dungaree with contrasting adjustable straps, the brownie suit of the 1890s was eventually sold for girls also. It was designed to protect good clothes and allow for practical activity. Today's overalls are not so far removed from those of 1905.

Drawers: This example, from around the 1820s, is made in cotton with muslin frills. Early drawers were often made with a bodice, this is a very shallow one, to keep them in place under high waisted dressers. The decorated hems would show beneath a short skirt.

Dungarees: See **dungaree dress** and adult **dungarees** for a fuller description. This example has button-through legs for ease of changing and adjustable straps for a good fit.

Bathing Suit (Boy's): This example is for small boys. Usually navy blue in colour, occasionally in red and generally made in wool, it was worn early in the twentieth century.

Bathing Suit (Girl's): This example was worn in the early twentieth century also and was more feminine in approach with puffed sleeves, gathering on to the yoke and the waist band, finished with frills at the knee.

Turkish Trousers/Bloomers: It was the sport of cycling that made divided skirts or full bloomers acceptable for girls. Two styles were available, the flared culotte and the full bloomer called Turkish trousers, both had the appearance of skirts rather than trousers. The bloomer style was gathered or pleated around the waist and gathered into a band below the knee.

Cardigan: Popular item, even today, to add an extra layer for warmth when necessary, see **knitted pram set** for popularity of knitwear.

Matinée Jacket: Popular style of knitted jacket for babies (see also **knitted pram set**).

Page 55

Christening Robe: Traditional dress reminiscent of long clothes – see **swaddling set with sleeves** – the dress is always very long, about one metre, and is usually made in lace and lined.

Christening Bonnet and Shoes: Matching accessories, again made in lace, to finish the christening outfit.

Embroidered Shawl: A fringed and embroidered shawl, highly decorated, used to wrap the baby during chilly church christenings.

Hussar Tunic: This tunic, from around 1930, has a split front and matching trousers. The set was worn both indoors and outdoors. This example has detachable sleeves.

Figaro Jacket/Suit: Another decorative suit similar to the exotic Zouave suit – see **Zouave suit**.

Norfolk Suit: This suit was made in fine fawn wool around 1878. These suits were designed for country wear and anticipated the more tailored styles of the 1890s. It has the typical pleated front and belt but is teamed with a pleated skirt.

Kate Greenaway Inspired Dress: Kate Greenaway (1846–1901) illustrated books with pictures that inspired a long-lasting cult for dressing children, beginning in the 1890s. The empire line, ankle length dresses were disapproved of in some areas of society as totally impractical but they were favoured by the artistic. She separated children's fashion from adult fashion. Her designs and use of fabrics were simple and long lasting. The Greenaway styles were never generally adopted but they still have influence today in party wear and bridesmaids wear, even down to the use of delicately sprigged floral prints. The style was popularised again in the 1970s by Laura Ashley.

Dress with Pantaloons: Long empire line dress with pantaloons showing intentionally beneath the dress, trimmed with lace around the hems and the neckline.

Page 56

Nightgown: this is a raglan-sleeved nightgown for babies from 1939 made in silk crepe.

Fishwife Draped Overskirt: Around 1880–1885 the fishwife style of dress became popular for girls. The overskirt was part of the bodice and the skirt underneath was often made from a different fabric, the overskirt is occasionally gathered up at the front as well as the back. This example shows no distinction between the under and overskirt. See also **shaped apron/sash**.

Princess Dress (Two Variations): Long-waisted dresses in the 1900s were referred to as princess dresses and were similar to those worn in the 1880s. Wide collars or ruffle-edged yokes gave their up-to-date appearance.

The skirt was referred to as a flounce. Pastel ribbons could be added for special occasions, but many dresses had no belt or sash of any sort. The longer example with pleated hem and side drapery shows the beginning of the revived bustle of the 1880s.

Overdress (Velvet): Pinafore style dress with long sleeves meant as a coverall and worn with a blouse underneath.

Slip/Baby Dress: When a baby was no longer swaddled it would wear a dress like this slip which originates from the mid eighteenth century and is made from coarse, block-printed linen. Printing meant the dirt would not show so easily, consequently the need for less frequent washing. Soap had a tax levied upon it.

Baby's Pelisse: Pelisses were originally coats made of dark silk, cut like a dress but open down the front. In the 1830s pelisses were made also in lightweight cottons for wear in the summer and are sometimes indistinguishable from dresses. This example is trimmed with a pleated ribbon and is double-breasted for extra warmth.

Shepherd's Smock: The Aesthetic Movement inspired the shepherd's smock style of dress dated around 1890. The garment was embellished by smocking and embroidery.

Page 57

Dress and Pant: This dress has smocking details and puffed sleeves with a small collar. The matching briefs, by hiding nappies, finish the outfit which is worn as much by babies today as in the past.

Sailor Suit: Sailor suits, or 'middies' as they were also termed, were accepted by every member of the family. They were popular from around the 1870s. The jacket would be the same style as that worn by boys but the trousers would be replaced by a pleated skirt. These suits reflected the growing popularity of seaside holidays among the middle classes. Long seaside visits necessitated the need for clothes that would stand up to the sun and salt water. Seaside resorts were seen as fashionable in the 1860s and 1870s and what was worn there was an influence on the rest of fashionable life. See also **sailor suit** for boys for the origin of the fashion.

Reefer Suit: Reefer suits were worn by boys and girls. This is a girl's version with scalloped, eyelet pique embellishment.

Buster Brown Suit (US)/Russian Suit/Military Blouse: This suit, often seen with the short knickerbockers as here, is thought to be inspired by Teddy Roosevelt's mediation in the Russian/Japanese War of 1905.

Consisting of a high-necked over blouse and knickers, the suits were worn by boys from the age of two-and-a-half to six years. They opened down the front, at the side front under one of the pleats, or at the back.

Tunic and Trousers: These tunics were appreciated by parents who wished to have a very gradual change from babyhood to boyhood. The slit down the front allowed the trousers to be seen. Often made in natural calico, the tunic was usually calf length and was worn around the early 1820s.

Little Lord Fauntleroy Suit: The story of Little Lord Fauntleroy was serialised in America in 1885 and published in book form in 1886. Written by the Anglo-American novelist, Frances Hodgson Burnett, the book was a great success. The fashion had already appeared in Britain. The suit was part of a fancy dress tradition evident previously in children's clothes, through, for example, the sailor suit and Scottish kilt. The suit consisted of jacket and knickerbockers in velvet with a contrasting trim. It had a vandyke collar and cuffs made of or trimmed with lace.

Zouave Suit: The Crimean war inspired exotic braid trimmed fashions for small boys, as also did the American Zouave military uniforms. Girls wore exotic bolero suits. The jackets were often collarless.

Eton Collar Suit: The Eton suit was popular in Britain and America. This example has the short straight jacket with fitted long sleeves. The suit was actually based on the uniform of the school. The suit was imposed on small boys to wear up to the 1920s.

Skeleton Suit: From 1770, after the age of five, the young boy was dressed in the skeleton suit. This consisted of a frilled shirt and trousers, the trousers usually buttoned onto the shirt. A short, fitting jacket, with two rows of buttons from shoulder to waist would be worn on top of the shirt.

Page 58

Skeleton Suit with Ruff: See **skeleton suit**. This example is worn with a ruff and has the characteristic double row of buttons.

Baby's Skeleton Suit: A very small version of the suit, see **skeleton suit** for a full description. This example has pleats at the waistband giving fullness, it also has a button flap between the legs.

Norfolk Suit: This was a very popular suit worn by boys (1890–1895) and developed for girls. The pleats on Norfolk jackets were added to allow for movement during sporting activities such as shooting and fishing.

The matching knickers and jacket were generally made in Harris tweed.

School Boy's Suit: The suit is an adult design made small, maintaining the details such as square shoulders and lapels which contrast with the shorts. The suit is made of chunky fawn wool.

Young Boy's Suit: Printed linen suit from around 1770–1780, the breeches have a front flap and deep waistband. The back split would have been laced up.

Garibaldi Suit: Inspired by the Italian patriot Giuseppe Garibaldi and his small army of 'red shirts', these date from the 1850s and 1860s.

Sailor Suit: This sailor suit could also be referred to as the 'jack tar' or 'man o' war' suit. The sailor suit fashion was thought to have begun with the Winterhalter portrait of the five-year-old Prince of Wales in 1846.

Page 59

Oilskin/Plastic Mackintosh: Derived from a fisherman's oilskin and usually found in bright yellow to match the traditional sou'wester (can also be found in reds, blues and greens), the details are as the original adult version with stud fastenings.

Montgomery/Duffle Coat: Small version of the adult **duffle coat** – see entry for full description, the main feature being the toggle fastening.

Showerproof Coat: The same function as the Splash Suit but covers the torso only. It is made in showerproof cire and is very lightweight so that it is easily carried for use when needed. It has a drawstring hem for further protection against the weather.

Djellabah: Made of coarse cotton this garment originates from North Africa around Morocco. The hooded top has ball decorations and gussets under the arms, it is of a very simple cut.

Hooded Anorak: A wind resistant and water repellent jacket which has elasticated cuffs for a good fit and a drawstring hem, this example has a concealed zip with stud fastenings for extra protection.

Sleeping Bag/Shelter Bag: A hooded dressing gown with ribbed cuffs, it has a detachable hem for warmth which buttons into place.

Korean Child's Jacket: This short jacket has tie fastens and is made in yellow taffeta lined with gauze.

Page 60

Carrying Cape: This is a two-tier carrying cape or cloak used to carry babies outside for air, they were meant to be seen when draped over the nurse's arms, made around 1870 this cape is deep blue wool trimmed with quilted white silk and tassels.

Hooded Circular Cloak with Ball Fringe: Two circles of fabric layered, create this cloak, decorated with a ball fringe, the cloak would have been draped around babies in cold weather.

Scalloped Cloak/Sack: This style of cloak was worn by toddlers and children up to the age of twelve. It was cut in eight sections, each section ending in a scallop. There is a stand-up collar at the neck and front button fastening, the body of the coat is called a sack.

Korean Dress: This dress is made from many colours of silk and is lined with calico, it has insets at the side to give a flared appearance.

Siberian Anorak: A fur trimmed leather jacket, with a split in the front seam, it has decorative embroidery around the sleeve and hem.

Highwayman Coat: Around 1895–1900 the highwayman coat became popular for girls and boys alike, derived from the adult version. The coats were frequently seen in bottle green or claret coloured broadcloth, with a stand-up collar in black velvet. Small boys would still wear the Little Lord Fauntleroy suit in black velvet.

Page 61

Fleecy Playsuit: This playsuit has sleeves and knitted cuffs for comfort. The zip is shaped to run down the inside of one leg to allow for extra access when changing nappies. The feet in this example have waterproof soles.

All-in-one (Hooded): A suit made in a warm fleecy fabric with knitted cuffs and button-through legs for ease of changing, for general day wear. Reminiscent of the Siren Suit worn during the Second World War, these were designed to be pulled on quickly during air raids in the night.

Padded Snowsuit: A snug all-in-one suit with fur trim and a layer of padding for warmth, in this example there are two zips for ease of dressing and undressing and knitted cuffs for a good fit in cold weather.

Playsuit: This example consists of a fleecy sweater under a sleeveless all-in-one, cut generously for active play. During the 1950s a fantasy element became apparent in the dressing of small boys in play suits inspired by cowboys, Indians and Davy Crockett. There was also interest in space technology reflected in knitwear such as 'jet plane' helmets with ear flaps.

Splash suit: A lightweight waterproof suit designed to fit over clothes and protect from wet weather. It has an elasticated waist for comfort and zip fastener.

MENS/WOMENSWEAR

Outerwear
Page 62

Burka/Cloth Mantle: A thick mantle/cloak worn everywhere in the Caucasus, made from felt-like woollen fabric, with tie fronts.

Mantle: A circular cloak, heavily embroidered in silk on satin, from the early 1600s, influenced by Spanish fashion but of German origin.

Page 63

Cape with Buttons: Cape of Spanish origin from 1630 to 1640, it has a multi-button fastening at the front and the sleeves are buttoned on also.

Djellabah: A type of cloak from North Africa and the Near East, it has long, wide sleeves. There are many variations on the name of this garment depending on the language of the country.

Garde de Corps with Hanging Sleeves: A thirteenth-century French cloak with side and full hanging sleeves, see also **hanging sleeve**.

Poncho Cape (Hooded): A waterproof cape, usually cut as one circle or square with a hole in the centre for the head, this example is updated with a contrasting hood, yoke and pockets. See **poncho**.

Page 64

Box Coat/Coachman's Coat: A coachman's overcoat worn when sitting on the box of a coach. It was heavy and loose fitting with or without capes.

Incroyable Coat: Incroyable is French for 'unbelievable' and described the dandy of the Directoire period (1795–1799). He made a cult of extremes in dress. This coat has a very neat waist and over-large lapels. The coat was worn with a **bicorne** (See ACCESSORIES – Hats) and bulky cravat. He would peer at people through his quizzing glasses.

Cut-Away Coat: A fitted coat with the skirt front almost totally cut away, manufactured in unfinished worsted.

Polonaise Style Coat with Brandenburg Fastenings: The polonaise was an eighteenth-century gown with a boned bodice fastened at the neckline. It was cut away at the waist to reveal a waistcoat. This coat takes its style from the gown. Brandenburg fastenings were ornamental, frog-like fastenings on outerwear.

Tail Coat: Part of formal or evening dress. There are tails falling down the back normally from the waist seam.

Page 65

Car Coat: A short coat which can be made in a plain fabric or, later on, in a checked fabric. The coat is straight in fit and is single breasted.

Western Horse Coat: A full and flaring coat with a gusset in the back to protect the wearer when horse riding in foul weather.

Crombie: The common name which is short for 'Abercrombie'. The garment is made in wool, usually dark in colour, with a contrasting bright lining. It has a concealed placket button fastening.

Page 66

Classic 1960s: A princess line, shorter length coat, made popular by Jackie Onassis (formerly John F. Kennedy's wife). She was considered a style icon in the 1960s and was emulated all over the world.

1920s Coat: This wool coat, with fur trim, would be worn with the cloche hat and is typical of the period.

Afghan: This coat was one of the commonest fashions in the 1970s worn by both sexes – unisex! The shaggier looking the better!

Early Motoring Coat: This full length coat covered as much clothing as possible. Roads at the turn of the twentieth century were dusty and dirty, it provided much needed protection and would be accompanied by goggles and a veiled hat.

Page 67

Kimono: The kimono is derived from a shift-like undergarment and lacks any form of individual tailoring or fastening. Twelve kimonos layered and worn for formal occasions are known as junihitoe. The spread of pattern over the surface is designed to wrap the wearer in bands of diagonal decoration.

Page 68

Furisode: From the 1700s this example was made of silk damask. The garment was a long-sleeved mourning garment worn frequently by priests in Japan.

Manga: A Mexican coat from the nineteenth century, which is cut in an oval with a slit to put the head through.

The name means sleeve.

Kalmuck Priest's Collar: A cape-like collar worn by the Kalmuck priests of the Caspian Steppes. It is made from Chinese silk with decorative edges.

Sarape: A sarape is part of the better class of Mexican dress, it is a type of poncho worn as a shoulder covering or coat.

Page 69

Capothe: A goat hair coat decorated with cord from Greece. The sleeves are open under the arm and the front is slightly cut away.

Siberian Hooded Coat: From the Northern region of the Yenisei river in Siberia, this hooded coat is made from reindeer skin and is decorated with fur and felt appliqué. It is slipped over the head with an opening in the neck to the right side, concealed by the construction seam.

Siberian Smock: A smock for men with the usual hood. Made from lightly tanned leather, the inside is especially soft. The coat has interesting construction lines, presumably governed by the size of the skins available.

Page 70

Burka and Mesh Eye-Piece/Chadri: A Middle Eastern cloak draped to cover a women's body completely. The eye-piece allows the wearer to see out.

Hayk: An oblong piece of cloth, often striped, which Arabs wrapped around their head and bodies over their clothes. Approximately six yards (5.5 m) in length.

Pelisse: A woman's mantle worn during the eighteenth century, usually fur lined and trimmed. It has a large collar or shoulder cape and occasionally a hood. The length varied from hips to ankles and there were slits for the hands.

Witchoura: A warm winter coat from 1808 until the 1830s, worn by women over the lightweight dresses of the period. It was fur trimmed and lined and named from a Polish wolf-skin coat called the wilczura. An ankle length garment, it had the fashionable high waistline of the time.

Page 71

Half Redingote: A woman's lightweight overcoat with a fitted bodice. It buttoned to the waist and was open from waist to hem, worn for riding or travelling, sometimes with a half skirt from side to side round the back. It was popular from the eighteenth century until the end of the nineteenth.

Paletot: A full skirted coat worn over crinolines and trimmed with velvet bands, often with shoulder capes, popular in the late 1880s.

Cocoon: A cocoon or barrel shaped coat, here with raglan sleeves in a contrasting fabric.

Redingote: A close fitting coat with a full skirt flaring from the waist. Redingote is the French adaptation of a 'riding coat' reimported into English fashion and was often worn by coachmen.

Page 72

Slicker: A waterproof raincoat with storm flaps, often worn at sea.

Goller: A woman's shoulder cape.

Visite: A sleeveless cape or mantle, fashionable in the late nineteenth century.

Steamer Coat: A warm overcoat, usually made from calf skin and belted at the waist.

Short Fitted Coat: A knee-length coat, quite fitted and with raglan sleeves, usually worn by women, this example has a woman's fastening.

Princess Line Coat: The construction lines of this coat are close fitting to the waist and flare out towards the hem.

Page 73

Duster: A light, loose fitting summer overcoat, usually quite long and acts as a clothing protector against dust.

Swagger: A full and flaring single-breasted woman's coat, here with raglan sleeves and slanted welt pockets.

A-Line Coat: Popular in the 1950s (this example) and with variations in the 1960s. This example is double breasted and is buttoned to the neck. The silhouette is like an 'A'.

Wrapover/Clutch: A straight overcoat with a double-breasted wrap but no buttons to fasten.

Page 74

Yakut Woman's Apron and Coat: Worn by women living around the mouth of the river Lena in Siberia. The coat is made from reindeer fur, with the hair side worn on the inside of the garment. The garments have cloth, velvet strips and glass pearl decoration.

Heuke with Hat (Back View): A cloak made from a rectangular piece of cloth draped over the head and over the shoulders which was held in place with a hat.

This garment was worn in Holland in the late 1500s and in various other parts of Europe and the Near East.

Page 75

Mantelet (Fur Trimmed): Worn from the Middle Ages onwards, mainly by women, this was very popular in the nineteenth century as outdoor wear with crinolines. It is usually a short mantle or sleeveless cape which covers the shoulders. This example is fur trimmed.

Ropa/Vlieger/Marlotte: High necked garment, fastening at the neck with a single decorative gem. The cap effect sleeve is padded and the garment flares out toward the hem. Worn by women in the sixteenth and early seventeenth centuries and thought to be of oriental origin. The garment was named and interpreted differently from country to country. It was made of velvet or silk and was often richly decorated.

Medieval Cloak (Hooded): Full cloak with decorative slits for the hands to pass through.

Page 76

Cape: Worn by both sexes, the cape is sleeveless and can be cut as a circle or flared, varying from very short to very long in length and anything in between.

Hoike: Cape, open on one side and fastened with buttons and hooks.

Balmacaan: A flared coat with flared sleeves. This coat was waterproof made in gabardine or tweed fabric.

Abayeh/Aba: Aba is the name of a coarse woollen fabric. The fabric is used to make a simple, usually striped, loose gown worn over other garments. It is worn in North Africa, Arabia, Turkey and Iran (Persia). The upper classes would wear the same style made in silk.

Page 77

Taglioni Coat: A braid-trimmed overcoat, named after the Italian dancer, Taglioni, usually with a checked lining.

Inverness Cloak: A sleeveless cloak with cape or capes draping from the shoulder. It is usually belted and made in a checked woollen fabric from Inverness, popular around the 1880s. The definition of a cloak is a loose outer garment falling from the neck and shoulders.

Academic Gown: A full-length black gown with flowing sleeves, not unlike the garde corps.

Usually worn with a **mortar board** and **hood cape** which is draped over the shoulders, see Accessories – Hats. Worn by graduates of colleges and universities and honoured celebrities on official academic ceremonies. Variations in design indicate the level of academic achievement, i.e. bachelor, master or doctor.

Shoulder Cape Coat: The coat is fitted to the waist then flares out at the hem, it has a shoulder cape for extra protection from the weather. The coat fastens to the waist only.

Page 78

Trench Coat: A coat worn by both sexes, a loose top coat, usually belted and made in cotton gabardine. It was originally worn by British officers in World War I, hence the name.

Frock Coat: A coat fitted to the waist with skirts hanging to the back of the knees, always from a waist seam, and maintaining this length all the way round.

Chesterfield: A knee length overcoat (as worn by the Earl of Chesterfield who lived in the eighteenth century) usually with a velvet collar and side flap pockets.

Cycle Mac: 'Mac' was an abbreviation for Charles Mackintosh who designed the raincoat and patented the first waterproofing process in 1823. The cycle mac is circular in cut to protect the cyclist and drapes over arms and handlebars, with a drawstring hood.

Loden: A waterproof cloth made by Tyrolean peasants which is woven from the fleeces of mountain sheep, and is characteristically dark green in colour. It gives its name to this coat.

Page 79

Ulster: Usually a double-breasted heavy overcoat with a half belt, it was worn by Irish men and women in Ulster. The cloth from which it is made also originated in Ulster.

Mackintosh: See **cycle mac.** A simply shaped garment with hood, belted and with large patch pockets, made from waterproof fabric for use in the rain.

Duffle/Montgomery: A felted fabric coat, usually around thigh length with toggle buttons and frog type fastenings. Worn and made famous by Field Marshall Montgomery in World War II, the duffle coat was said to have originated from the Navy when worn as protection from stormy seas.

Gabardine Raincoat: Gabardine is a cotton or rayon fabric in which the fibres are waterproofed before weaving. The name is also given to the garments which are manufactured from it. The coat consists of wide raglan sleeves and is fastened at the centre front, often with a concealed placket (as here) and sometimes belted.

Page 80

Noh Costume: Worn by Japanese actors around 1680, usually elaborately decorated and made from silk or satin.

Chinese Shoulder Cape: A square-shaped shoulder cape worn with the points down the back, front and over the shoulders. Made from silk brocade, the garment was worn for ceremonies over other garments.

Szur Coat: A shepherd's coat from Hungary made from woollen blanket fabric, with elaborate contrasting embroidery. The coat has an extra deep collar.

Page 81

Jaronga/Poncho: The primitive name for this poncho is 'jaronga' and this example is derived from Mexico in the nineteenth century. The poncho (see also Jackets) is a square or rectangle of fabric with an opening cut in the middle for the head. It may be fastened at the sides.

Korean Overcoat: Made from Chinese damask this Korean overcoat has contrasting ribbon ties to fasten and an interesting cut to the sleeve.

Jackets
Page 82

Double-Breasted (Woman's Fastening): This jacket has a wrap-over enabling two sets of buttons to fasten either side of the centre front.

Single-Breasted (Woman's Fastening): This jacket fastens with one row of buttons down the centre front, it also fastens on the woman's side, that is, right over left.

Basque: The jacket skirt is an extension of the bodice, giving a fit and flare silhouette. The sleeves are cut flared to the wrist. The basque is probably derived from Basque dress in Spain.

Spencer: This garment has been attributed to Lord Spencer, who claimed fashion as absurd. He produced this very short, waisted jacket to be worn with the empire line dresses of the late 1700s.

Bolero: This is a short loose fitting jacket with the fronts curved slightly away. It originates from Spain and is similar to the toreador's jacket.

Blazer: Originally for boating or cricketing, this garment is now worn for many occasions usually in the summer. It is a lightweight, often flannel, jacket that can be plain or striped. This example is womenswear with its slight shaping and woman's fastening. For men the cut would be less fitted.

Casual Jacket: A contemporary, soft jacket, made in a velvet for a luxurious feel, worn for day wear.

Shawl: The shawl can be varying sizes of a rectangle or triangle, usually with a fringed edge, and in any fabric. The shawl drapes over the neck and shoulders.

John Galliano Jacket: Now a famous designer, this was one of Galliano's early designs, the cut of the collar/hood is notable.

Cape: A contemporary decorative fabric drape worn to dress-up jackets and coats similar in function to the tippet.

Maternity: Prior to the twentieth century maternity wear was not specifically designed, garments being usually adapted by adding lace-up fronts. This jacket has adjustable buttons and ribbon ties.

Page 83

Caraco: During the eighteenth century women wore jackets which were the same design as their gowns but were cut off at the hip. The jackets were very full in the skirt but were rather cut-away at the front.

Cardigan Jacket: Generally a knitted garment with centre front button fastening. It originated from the Earl of Cardigan who wore a short, knitted worsted military jacket.

Stole: A long rectangular piece of cloth, often fringed at the ends, worn wrapped around the shoulders, not dissimilar to the shawl.

Hussar: A short, cut-away jacket worn by women, popular around 1813 after the Peninsular War. The jacket is made more feminine with its fur trim, but keeps the frog effect decoration.

Pashmina: A stole, often in cashmere, that became popular in the late 1990s, worn over coats and jackets.

Peplum: This jacket has a full circular cut skirt, quite short in length, hanging from the waist seam.

Canezou: A short fur trimmed jacket without sleeves for women.

Tyrolean/Loden: Loden is the fabric, see Outerwear – **Loden**, the Tyrolean jacket has a braid trim and originates from traditional Tyrolean dress from Austria.

Chanel/Box: This hip length, boxy shaped jacket was designed by Coco Chanel. For women it is usually worn with a skirt in the same fabric and has the Chanel hallmarks of braid trimmed edges, welt pockets and gilt buttons.

Tippet: An historic and contemporary, fake fur collar worn to dress-up jackets or coats, often with a brooch to fasten.

Hacking/Riding: This jacket is worn with jodhpurs for horse riding. It is a fitted jacket with a slightly flared skirt, often with contrasting yoke and elbow patches.

Page 84

Shirt: slightly heavier than a normal shirt, this jacket has the same features. A loose garment for men and boys worn under a coat, it still has the curved tails of a normal shirt.

Barbour™/Gamekeeper/Fowler/Shooting/Fishing: Barbour is the trade name for this jacket, normally manufactured in a thorn-proof fabric, usually waxed for wet weather. It is a very hard wearing jacket with multiple pockets and can be fleece lined for extra warmth. It is also worn by women.

Sports: A loosely cut jacket in tweed or cotton, normally checked.

Teddy Boy/Drape: These were long drape jackets trimmed with velvet, echoing Edwardian styling (hence the 'Teddy Boy' name) and worn with drainpipes, brothel creepers and bootlace ties.

Mess: Officers of the armed forces wear this jacket on formal occasions. The colour depends on the tradition of the regiment or corps.

Sailor/Pea: A heavy jacket worn by American sailors, normally dark navy in colour.

Smoking: Originally a jacket for lounging informally at home and usually made in rich brocade or velvet fabrics, this garment was typified by Noel Coward.

Page 85

Denim: Derived from the western cowboy style and made in denim because it is hard wearing. Denim is an abbreviation for 'de Nimes', the French city from which the fabric is said to have originated. The heavy orange top-stitching is also a hallmark of this classic cult garment.

Naval Reefer: A semi-fitting Navy jacket, usually double-breasted and fastened with brass or military type buttons.

Camouflage Smock/Combat: Worn by the armed forces. The camouflage pattern can change from jungle greens to sandy yellows depending on where the jacket is to be worn. The jacket has multiple pockets on the sleeves as well as the front of the garment, and also has epaulettes on the shoulders. There is a drawstring waist and hem, Velcro™ cuffs and button-through front.

Bomber: A waist length blouson with knitted cuffs, collar, waistline and welt pockets.

Gas Jacket: A warm fleece lining for the fishtail parka worn on its own as a collarless jacket popular in the late 1970s.

Biker: The motorbike jacket has gone from being a protective garment to be being a cult object. Mostly designed in black leather with many zipped pockets, the jacket sometimes has a quilted lining in bright red fabric and is slightly longer than waist length for extra protection to the cyclist.

Chinese Workwear: This modern Chinese work jacket became a uniform for the Chinese.

Page 86

Continental Sack Coat (Man's Fastening): A short, loose, masculine jacket, this example is from Europe.

Capelet: A short cape without sleeves draping around the shoulders.

Embroidered: This elaborately decorated jacket, or coat as it is better known, was probably worn for ceremonial occasions. Dated around the early eighteenth century.

Tuxedo: A dinner jacket normally black or midnight blue in colour, often with a silk collar, this originated as a less formal jacket for small dinners and was modified by American millionaires living in Tuxedo Park, New York.

Ivy League: A masculine sack coat, observed at Yale, Harvard and Princeton universities and smaller colleges. The jacket has natural shoulders, narrow lapels, and is straight and unpadded.

Waiter's: This jacket is normally made from white cotton and is slightly double-breasted. It has pointed fronts and is worn by waiters in smart restaurants.

Carmagnole: A short jacket worn by the 'sans culottes' of the French Revolution in 1792, it was derived from a workman's jacket worn in Carmagnola in Italy. It was adopted by revolutionaries in Marseilles and then Paris.

Sack Coat: see the **continental sack coat**.

Bell Boy (US)/Page Boy: A short fitted jacket that is single breasted but has two extra rows of buttons from the shoulder to the waist, the front of the jacket dips into a point.

Page 87

Donkey: This jacket is regularly worn by British workmen. It is usually black with a deep, waterproof yoke running down the back. It has a concealed button fastening.

Cycling: A lightweight cycling jacket made from fabric that wicks away moisture, it is quite long in the body for comfort when cycling. It has elasticated cuffs and hem for protection against the wind and a large back pocket for carrying small items.

Norfolk: A mid-thigh length jacket with box pleats on each front and in the centre of the back. It has inverted pleat pockets and a self-belt and is often made in Harris tweed.

Varsity (US)/Blouson: 'Varsity' is an abbreviation of university. This jacket is of American origin and is also known as an American College Blouson. The jacket body is usually made in a heavy wool fabric and the sleeves in leather. College football team names are often embroidered on the jacket. The cuffs and waist are made from knitted ribs, often with coloured stripes running through them.

Shell: The shell jacket is a sports jacket made in a lightweight breathable fabric, usually made up as a series of colour blocks or stripes in bright colours. It is worn with co-ordinating trousers and is known as a **shell suit** see Suits. The silhouette is that of the jogging top or track-suit jacket.

Fishtail Parka: A waterproof jacket for inclement weather normally with a fur-trimmed hood, drawstring waist and hem. The 'fishtail' allows the drawstring to be tightened around the legs for extra protection. The jacket is worn by Inuit, the armed forces and sometimes becomes a fashion item.

Page 88

Military: Derived from the Hussar jacket at the time of the Crimean War (the Hussar being a lightly armed cavalry soldier). It is heavily braided and buttoned.

Battle: A waist length, single-breasted jacket worn by the armed forces, it has a wrap-around self-belt.

Mackinaw Cruiser (US): Worn by lumbermen and hunters with many utility pockets. Mackinaw is the fabric that the jacket is made from, it is heavy and woollen and napped on both sides so that no weave is visible on the surface, but is often woven in large checks.

Western/Bietle: Usually made from suede, the main feature of this jacket is its fringing, the jacket probably originated from the native American Indian, whose jackets were made from deerskin and were called bietle jackets.

Nehru (Man's Fastening): An eastern, slightly fitted, tailored coat with a mandarin collar. This jacket fastens on the man's side, that is left over right.

Anorak: A wind resistant and water repellent jacket used in winter sports. It has a zip fastening with elasticated cuffs and drawstring hood and hem for a good fit.

Tracksuit: This jacket is often worn with matching trousers. It is a simple, hooded blouson shaped garment and is usually made from a fleece-backed fabric to keep the body warm while sports training.

Breathable Parka: The parka has drawstrings at the waist and hem and around the hood. It is made from a breathable but waterproof fabric for comfort.

Page 89

Ski Blouson: Worn for skiing and made for comfort, warmth and protection against the elements. This jacket has a double fastening front for extra protection.

Cagoule/Jack in a Pack™: A lightweight, waterproof garment, with a hood and elasticated cuffs and hem. Designed to keep out inclement weather as a covering over layers of other clothes. It can be rolled up when not in use and packed away into a carry pack.

Cropped Wading: A short waterproof jacket worn when fishing, it should be worn with waders or chest waders. It has a zip and stud fastening for comfort.

Golf/Harrington™: Harrington is the trade name for this jacket. The golf jacket is slightly blouson in silhouette, has knitted rib cuffs and waist, a stand collar and, usually, a checked lining.

Duvet/Down/Puffa: A wadded jacket quilted sparingly which resembles a duvet, meant for comfort and warmth.

Safari/Bush: A traditional African safari jacket, usually water repellent, it has garment, shell, breast and bellows pockets and is generally light in colour.

Flying: A leather, waist-length, blouson style jacket, worn by American flyers in World War II, usually fleece lined for warmth.

Page 90

Tschepken: A Kurdish jacket made in contrasting colours, that is, the lining, jacket and decoration. The jacket is popular from the Near East to Turkey, Greece and Bosnia.

Gheila/Tunisian Man's: This jacket should be worn with the **szedria** or **firmla** in Waistcoats.

It is decorated with braid and has metal buttons on the lower sleeve.

Colley Westonward: This is actually a term meaning 'worn awry', and is a way of wearing the Mandilion. The side seams being open allows the Mandilion to be swung round with the sleeves hanging down the back and front of the body.

Mandilion: A hip length loose jacket with open side seams, often with braid trim.

Cotehardie: A tunic worn by both men and women from the late twelfth to the fourteenth century. This example is fur lined and has hanging sleeves with slits for the arms.

Burmese Jacket: The projecting side flaps over the hips are typical of Burmese shaping along with a rectangular panel behind the front opening. The jacket has a 'twisted rope' design that is also typically Burmese. The fabric is quilted cotton embroidered with silk.

Page 91

Shober: A garment worn by the Chuvash people from the Volga. It is made from coarse linen and has a full skirt at the sides. The front and back panels are quite flat.

Kamishimo: Part of the costume of a Samurai from Japan, the garment is very wide at the shoulders and folds at the waist.

Siberian Man's: The garment is made from fur, the hem border from mosaics of fur. There is a flap hanging down at the front from the hood.

Poncho: A rough woollen square of fabric with a hole in the centre for the head, originating from the South American Indian, it is brilliantly coloured and patterned.

Waistcoats
Page 92

Grossera Skin Coat: A short coat worn by men in the mountainous district of the Yemen, made out of skins with leather trimming.

Aba: The ordinary aba consists mainly of brown and white stripes, the shoulder seam, centre seam, horizontal strips across the chest and slit for the neck are embroidered in brightly coloured silk. See also Outerwear – **Abayeh/Aba.**

Surcoat: This is a term used to describe the top tunic worn by either sex during the Middle Ages. This example was worn by women and has cut-away sides and a totally button-through front.

Tabard: A ceremonial or military top worn from the thirteenth to the sixteenth century. A very simple garment, it pulls over the head and is open at the sides, see also **Tabard** in Dresses.

Under Doublet: This was worn with or without sleeves, for extra warmth or to display rich fabrication. The garment was fitted to the waist then flared out, buttoning through the front and with a deep vent in the back.

Page 93

Pelerine: A women's short garment of the nineteenth century, here without sleeves, made of silk, velvet or fur.

Gilet: A contemporary waistcoat lined with fake fur, the seams are also trimmed with fur, available in rich, deep colours.

Szedria/Firmla: A cloth waistcoat which has a matching jacket see **gheila.** This waistcoat buttons through the front on an extended placket and has bound edges.

Tattersall Check: Classic waistcoat silhouette made in a Tattersall check (the name is derived from the New-market saleroom for racing stock), which normally has narrow lines crossing closely together. Single-breasted fastenings have the buttons and buttonholes placed on the centre front with a slight button wrap added (usually the diameter of the button plus seam allowance).

Dress: A fitted waistcoat with shawl collar worn with evening dress, this is similar to the classic shape but with richer fabrication and in sombre colours.

Crocheted: This waistcoat was crocheted – a ubiquitous 1970s feature.

Duvet: Similar to the duvet jacket but without sleeves.

Classic: The shape, nowadays, changes very subtly but is usually single-breasted with welt pockets. The bottom button should not be fastened. The straight back is often in a contrasting fabric with self-belt that is adjustable, the fronts dip into points.

Longline: This design was from the Biba boutique in London, manufactured in a rich, brocade fabric.

The original designer and founder of Biba was Barbara Hulanicki.

Aspen Vest (US): The Aspen vest is usually suede with fur trim for warmth, it has large pockets with rouleau fastenings and a yoke. Common in America.

Logger's/Cruiser/Utility: Similar to the mackinaw jacket but without sleeves, it has shell pockets (for carrying shotgun cartridges).

English Hunting: Normally made in Harris tweed, this waistcoat has a very square, boxy shape with side splits and slightly lower back.

Double-breasted: The fronts are extended to form a wrap and two rows of buttons are balanced either side of the centre front.

Trousers
Page 94

Hot Pants: See **Hot pants with bib**.

Pleated Shorts with Turn-ups: These are woven shorts with un-pressed pleats at the front for comfort, the shorts also have a fly front and turn-ups.

Jams (US): An American beach fashion derived from pyjamas and always printed with florals.

Jogging: Shorts designed for jogging, with an elasticated waist and binding around the hem. The hem is curved upwards at the side seams.

Lederhosen: A German expression for shorts held up by crossbar leather braces. The shorts are of leather also and worn in the Tyrol as traditional dress.

Cycling Shorts: A stretch Lycra™ short that is more of a fashion item than true sports short, it is not padded or heavily constructed.

Trunk Hose and Cannons/Canions: 'Trunk hose' is the term for the garment which extended from the waist to the thigh before the word breeches came into use in the Middle Ages. Cannons or canions were the extension to the hose which fit the thigh to the knee.

Rehearsal Shorts: A fitted short with flaring hems, made in a stretch fabric for comfort during dance rehearsals. Nowadays leotards and short shorts have usurped rehearsal shorts.

Eight Panel Cycling Shorts: A true cycling short constructed for the sport, the panels are shaped for the position in the saddle. Made in stretch fabric and usually with a padded crutch area.

Shorts with Built-in Briefs: These shorts have a built in brief for support.

Beach Bloomers: A full short controlled by bands at the hems which are around the top of the thigh.

Short Shorts: Very skimpy shorts, here with a slightly high waist and cut-away legs.

Athletic Shorts with Bib: A stretch short with bib for men's athletics. The leg finishes mid thigh and the back view shows a racing back.

Slashed Trunk Hose: See **Trunk hose and cannons**. This garment is padded with horsehair and is slashed according to the fashion, 1520–1540. Slashing is said to have emerged after Swiss mercenaries defeated the Burgundians in 1477, they mended their tattered uniforms with strips of the banners and hangings from their enemy. An opposing theory is that the Lansquenet, Swiss and Bavarian mercenaries found their clothes too tight and so slashed them for comfort, but showed their tunics or shirts beneath. All garments received the treatment in 1520. The edges of the slashing were embroidered or braided and the garment beneath was pulled through to show contrast.

Hipsters: Low slung, contemporary shorts, in bright coloured print with decorative belt.

Shorts Skirt: Full, gathered shorts, having the appearance of a skirt, this example was made in a jersey fabric giving a more fluid appearance.

Culottes: This garment has the appearance of a skirt. Normally described as a divided skirt it was devised in the 1930s before shorts were acceptable for women.

Page 95

Trouser Skirt (Two Versions): A normal trouser with a second, top layer forming a skirt effect.

Bloomers: A full trouser meant for women, gathered in, above the ankles and at the waist, named after the American reformer, Amelia Jenks Bloomer.

Jogging Pants: Fleece backed interlock is used for comfort and warmth in this trouser. The trouser has an elasticated waist and knitted rib cuff.

Harem/Balloon: A full trouser on a shaped waistband. The full leg is controlled at the hem by elastication. The harem is usually made in a supple silk fabric.

Chalvar: An Afghan trouser that is a piece of cloth pulled up between the legs and tied around the waist creating a paperbag waistline.

Drawstring Braes/Bracchae: Iron Age tribal trousers. A simply cut trouser with drawstring waist and wrapped ankles.

Iranian Woman's Trouser (with Feet): A very full trouser controlled by a drawstring and with feet attached. Made from calico, usually with a floral pattern and worn by the woman when out of doors.

Page 96

Palazzo: An Italian expression for a woman's wide-legged trouser, the flaring begins at about hip level.

Gaucho: The uniform trouser of the Argentinian cowboy, adapted by women, quite wide in the leg.

Woman's Worksuit: The same principle as the jumpsuit, but here more feminine due to the styling, that is, the shaped waist and revers collar and cuffs. The garment zips open through the left side seam. It is made in a woven fabric and the pleats and blouson effect are for comfort when bending and stretching.

Hot Pants with Bib: The name given to sports shorts, popular in the early 1970s. Mr Freedom, the Pop Art designer, specialised in creating fun clothes – including hot pants. This example has the addition of a bib.

Bodysuit/Catsuit: A complete cover that hugs the body, consequently it is made in a stretch fabric with some Lycra™/elastane content. It is impossible to get this sort of fit from a woven fabric as there is no 'give'.

Leggings: A body-hugging trouser always made in a stretch fabric to get the desired fit, this may be a jersey or a Lycra content fabric. Leggings can be worn with tunics, baggy tops or short dresses.

Straight Tailored: Trousers that fit the wearer well and are shaped to fit. This example shows a fly front fastening but has a woman's proportions.

Capri: A trouser that finishes at mid-calf level and is quite fitted, made in a woven fabric.

Page 97

Slops Finished with Fringed Sashes: In the sixteenth and early seventeenth centuries 'slops' referred to the wide baggy breeches of the time. This example, drawn in at the waist, is finished at the knee with a fringed sash.

Slashed Breeches: See **slashed trunk hose**. From the late sixteenth century men wore breeches, an outer garment covering the hips and legs as far as the knee. These were eventually superseded by trousers in the nineteenth century.

One Piece Hose: The upper stocks are striped and the nether stocks are in two colours, giving a trompe l'oeil effect, the garment is actually made in one piece.

Rhinegrave/Petticoat Breeches: From the seventeenth century men wore breeches that were not gathered at the knee, instead they had ruffles, lace and ribbons for decoration.

Spanish Hose: Usually these trousers are decorated with braids or buttons.

Cloak Bag Breeches: An early seventeenth century trouser, this garment was oval in shape and was very full, drawn in a little above the knee and finished with lace or point decoration.

Under-Breeches: These were worn under the Rhinegrave breeches/petticoat breeches and were quite full, being restrained by a band at the knee.

Dhoti: Of Indian origin, this is a piece of cloth pulled up between the legs and fastened around the waist.

Brechs/Drawers: A trouser that could be 'drawn' on, normally a linen undergarment. This example finishes below the knee and is tied with wrap ties, the waist if very full and drawn up with ties.

Panung: A length of fabric that is passed between the legs and held at the waist with a belt. The fabric may hang between the knee and the ankle, it forms part of traditional Thai dress.

Page 98

Sans Culottes: This was the name given to the revolutionaries in France, around 1792, because they wore trousers rather than the fashionable knee breeches. The term means 'without trousers'. The trousers are of simple, straight cut with a fall front, for access, buttoned with two buttons.

Pedal Pushers: Trousers that fall to below the knee at mid-calf level, they are slightly loose and worn for cycling and sailing.

Bermudas: Shorts that finish just above the knee and are used for sports.

Pegged: The trousers have pleats at the waist creating a slightly rounded silhouette, the trouser leg tapers to the ankle.

Long Knee Breeches: A later seventeenth century fashion, originating in France, and lasting until after 1800. The breeches became skin tight and were cut on the bias to achieve this. The back was extended to a high waistline. At the front, the fabric stretched across the thighs and was either sewn or buttoned on to a wide waist hugging waistband. The trouser was pulled down over the stocking and buckled or buttoned in position. The fabric was often the same as the coat.

Fitted Breeches with Fall Front: A fall-front trouser which is quite fitted, as the long knee breeches.

Slim Jims/Drain Pipes: A narrow fitting trouser finishing at the ankle, this example would fasten at the back.

Jamaica Shorts: Fly-fronted shorts reaching mid-thigh length.

Toreador: This trouser is worn by Spanish bullfighters and is tight fitting and reaches below the knee.

Clam Diggers (US): 'Clam diggers' is an American expression. These trousers are wider than pedal pushers but are about the same length, they have a curved hem with notched effect at the side seams.

Army Fatigues: Worn by the armed forces, fatigues are sometimes worn by the public when sold by 'army surplus' stores. They are always khaki (the Hindi word for dust coloured).

Cargo: The cargo trouser is a derivation of army clothing, a development of the combat pant, which had also been popular, with its distinctive knee-high pockets.

Page 99

Hipsters: Fly-fronted trousers, the normal waistline has been dropped to just above the hipline, with the normal finishing of a band with belt loops.

Bondage Trousers with Bum Flap: Tight-fitting trousers with multiple zips, mostly decorative. The trousers have tabs with D-rings to attach bondage straps, a series of criss-cross straps fixed across the backs of the legs. Part of this attachment is the crescent shaped 'bum flap' which hangs from behind, usually in a contrast fur fabric, introduced by Vivien Westwood in the mid 1970s.

Oxford Bags: From the 1920s, these trousers were worn by English men and had very wide flared bottoms up to twenty-four inches (61 cm).

Knickerbockers: The name is derived from the fictional author Dietrich Knickerbocker in Washington Irving's *A History of New York*. Knickerbockers are baggy trousers finishing past the knee with a cuff to control the fullness.

Plus Fours: The term is believed to apply to breeches in the British Army when they were measured as reaching to the knee plus four inches. Plus fours are used for sportswear and are often checked. The loose fabric is drawn into a band below the knee.

Ski Pants: Usually made from a stretch fabric for comfort during skiing, the trousers have 'stirrups' around the feet.

Chinos: A popular trouser which takes its name from the fabric, 'chino', which is usually white, pure cotton, in twill or plain weave, and is hard wearing. The trouser is a classic shape with a fly front, and has jetted back and side pockets.

Baggy Jeans: A development of the denim jean, the silhouette became rounded and very loose fitting.

Page 100

Tailored with Turn-Ups: The same principle as the straight tailored trouser but here with turn-ups. Turn-ups are a deep hem of the trouser leg folded back so that the fabric face still shows.

Bell Bottoms: Originally worn by sailors, these 1960s trousers were not as wide and flared from the mid-calf.

Denim Jeans: Originally used for work-wear, the jean is a classic cult garment with fly front fastening, top-stitching, back yoke detailing and belt loops, traditionally indigo blue and made from cotton. Nowadays the jean can be many colours but the fabric is easily recognisable by the white yarn weft and coloured warp. It is a hard wearing fabric that can be treated to look 'worn', 'distressed', stone washed' or 'snow washed', or it can simply be allowed to fade naturally after washing.

Cigarette Pants (US): A narrow-legged pant with fly front and slanted inset pockets.

Tartan Trews: In the sixteenth century the Scots wore trews, as did the Irish. The trousers were always made in tartan, or plaid as it is also known.

Briar Pants: A work-wear trouser with a thorn-proof nylon layer from the thigh to the hem, it also has large pockets.

Loons: The wide flare from the knee epitomised the 1960s 'loon' pant, often patches and insertions were made in an attempt to add more flare.

Page 101

Northern Soul: An early 1970s exaggeration of the flared trouser. The trouser fitted the waist and hips and then reached the ground, often covering the shoe. There was multi-button detailing on the wide waistband. It is closely related to its predecessor, the Oxford bag, the hems of which occasionally reached twenty-four inches (61 cm) wide.

Flares: A normal, fitted, trouser shape to the knee, the leg then flares outward to the ankle.

Jodhpurs: Riding breeches originating from India, baggy to the knees and tight fitting from knee to ankle with re-inforcement patches for rigorous wear.

Apron-Like Trousers: Part of an officer's uniform from ancient China. The trouser is wrapped and tied around the waist, the decoration is appliquéd.

Lepsha Leggings: These leggings, from Darjeeling, were fastened to a girdle at the waist, similar to the Persian fashion.

Chaps: Short for 'chaparejos' and worn in Mexico, these leg coverings are the closed leg type called shotguns because they resemble twin gun barrels.

Page 102
Caspian Steppes (Woman's): A wide trouser with full panels between the legs and a drawstring waist.

Salopettes/Overalls/Boiler Suit: A loose garment worn over the top of normal clothing as a protection against dirt, normally with slits in the sides so that the pockets in the normal clothing are accessible. Salopettes are slightly different in that they may have shoulder straps only, like dungarees, and are meant as a coverall when skiing or during other sports. It is a French term.

Jumpsuit: Originally 'the siren suit' of World War II, which could be quickly put on during air raids at night, this example borrows more from the armed forces parachute jumping attire. It is a complete body cover with zip front fastening. Made in a woven fabric, the garment is baggy for ease of movement.

Gatya: Coarse linen trousers from Hungary, worn by men. They are a simple set of rectangles with a gusset between the legs and a drawstring waist. The trousers would be very full when fastened and hang just below the knee. They would be worn with boots. This is a side view.

Bib Shorts for Cycling: The shorts are constructed in panels that are shaped for comfort when cycling (see **eight panel cycling shorts**). Here, there is the addition of a bib for extra streamlining and comfort when cycling.

Page 103
Sarouel/Zouave: These trousers formed part of the uniform of the Zouave Regiment, originally formed of Kabyles (Berbers) of Algiers. The trouser has a dropped crutch as part of the gathered inset between the legs, making it very comfortable to wear. It is best made in a light jersey or similar fabric.

Ssernall Trousers: A full trouser from Egypt pulled together with a drawstring, the leg tapers to a tight ankle, but there is still a gusset between the legs for movement.

Slavian: Made from coarse linen, these trousers are cut in the South Slav fashion. They have a slight drawstring waist and slits for access. There is a gusset of interesting cut between the legs.

Hakama Trousers: This is a skirt-like trouser worn by Japanese men belted over the kimono. It is pre-nineteenth century.

Lapp Trousers: These trousers are worn by men and women in Lapland. Note the unusual cut of the trouser, there is no crutch seam between the legs.

Page 104
Fishing Leggings: Waterproof leggings that fasten by studs onto a wading jacket, over the top of day clothes.

Flying Suit: This suit has the same function as the jumpsuit. It originates from the armed forces and is a functional garment, shown here with zipped pockets and self-belt with buckle.

Siren Suit: See **jumpsuit** for full description.

Chest Waders: A waterproof trouser, usually made from rubber, that has built in boots for deep river fishing. There are adjustable straps for a good fit. The waders fit over the top of normal clothes.

Dungarees: A workman's overall with a bibbed front and adjustable straps, usually normal denim detailing, e.g. top-stitching and patch utility pockets. Made in denim recently, but originally made from a fabric called dungaree – consequently the name. Dungaree is hardwearing and made from cotton but the warp and weft threads are generally the same colour unlike denim where the weft is white and the warp coloured.

Suits
Page 105
Dress: This example is probably of French origin from around the 1790s. It would have been worn for ceremonial occasions and is decorated with elaborate silk embroidery. The coat, waistcoat and breeches are all made from the same fabric, the coat and waistcoat are the most elaborate.

Harlequin: A late sixteenth-century character in Italian comedy called Arlecchino wore a jacket and fitting trousers in a light coloured fabric with brightly coloured patches placed randomly to look like a tattered costume. Towards the seventeenth century the costume became more refined, the patches were arranged symmetrically and were confined to blue, red and green or white, red and green triangles. A feminine version, Arlecchina, appeared and she wore the same decoration on her costume.

Summer Formal: Dated around 1760, this suit is made from fine quality silk. It would probably have been worn in the summer for formal occasions. The coat, waistcoat and breeches are all made from the same fine fabric.

Parti-Coloured Dress and Harlot: A close fitting doublet and hose with the two legs joined together (i.e. tights) called 'harlot'. The doublet and hose are split into blocks and worked in two contrasting colours – this is parti-colouring. This example has integral leather soles.

Page 106

Chesterfield: This suit dates from around 1954 and is for women. See the description regarding the **Chesterfield coat**. The suit would be worn over a discreetly checked blouse at the races. Co-ordinating gloves, hat, umbrella and shoes would have completed the look.

Doublet, Breeches and Cloak: Dated around 1630 this suit consists of doublet, breeches and cloak. The fabric is slashed and braided satin. The outfit is typical of its period; the doublet is high-waisted and the breeches taper to the knee.

Catsuit: Manufactured in a slinky synthetic jersey this cat suit also carried the leopard skin print popular in the 1970s.

Nehru: Dating from the late 1960s this suit was inspired by the Nehru trend of the time. With the stand collar, multi-button fastening and slim styling, it is made in a pin stripe suiting.

Zoot Suit: Originating from the jazz culture of the southern states of America, this suit was popular in the 1940s and re-emerged briefly in the 1980s. The suit consisted of a knee length jacket, knee length watch chain and floppy trousers. It would be accessorised by a pork pie sombrero.

Trouser Suit: Trouser suits were very popular in the 1970s and were often made in Crimplene (heat treated polyester) which allowed for clear prints, prints were 1920/30s inspired. (Trousers on page 107.)

Page 107

Shell: See **shell jacket** for a full description.

Chanel: See **Chanel jacket** for full description.

Modern Chanel: A modern variation of the Chanel suit by Karl Lagerfeld. The designer is still using tweed but the shaping of the suit is updated with bra top, hipster mini and the incorporation of the corset, there is also a short jacket (not shown), making up a four piece.

Evening: This suit dates from the 1920s. Since the nineteenth century full evening suits were worn with a white

waistcoat instead of black; this is a more old fashioned version. The suit consists of a tail coat with silk lapels, slim trousers and a low cut waistcoat. It would be worn with a stiff fronted white shirt, a wing collar and white bow tie.

Trouser suit: see page 106.

Athletic outfit: A vest top and brief designed to be as streamlined as possible when used in athletics by women. The fabric would be a lightweight stretch and the construction lines give a feeling for shape.

Single-breasted: A generic example of a suit style that has many variations. The suit consists of a jacket and trouser and is fastened on the man's side. Waistcoats in the same fabric have been added and the fastening may change to double-breasted. Often made in a wool suiting for ceremonial and work occasions, or in summer weight fabrics, the possibilities and variations are endless.

Skirts
Page 108

Micro: Probably the shortest a skirt will ever get – just below the top of the thigh.

Mini: Normally mid-thigh length.

Midi: Normally mid-calf level with a button-through front, the buttons finishing at mid-thigh level to aid walking.

Maxi: Normally ankle length, with a button-through front finishing at mid-thigh to aid walking.

Floor Length/Dinner: Normally a floor-length skirt, this example has a wrap-over one-button fastening.

Ballerina: An ankle-length full skirt, not unlike the length of the ballerina dress.

Hobble/Pencil: The hobble is a very narrow, tapered, ankle-length skirt, impossible to walk in, so necessitating a side slit. The pencil skirt was of a similar shape but not as long. It usually had a vent in the back for walking.

Flared: This skirt is fuller than the A-line, the waist measurement remains the same but fullness is added in the cut of the two pieces so the hem circumference increases.

Gored and Flared: A gore is a panel of fabric that can be shaped at the sides to remove the necessity for darts, when put together with other panels the shape is retained. A gored skirt can have three, four, five, six, seven, eight or more gores. The example shown has six.

Circular: This example is one full circle, normally cut as two half circles with two seams. One and a half, two or three circles may be used. Each time a circle is added there will be more seams and the circumference of the hole in the middle of the circles, making up the eventual waistline, must be reduced to keep the waist measurement, as it is a feature of the construction that there are no darts.

Straight Fitted: This skirt has a high, bandless, faced waist with darts. The darts open out over the hips and as they move up under the bust, while at the waist they are taking in most of the fabric fullness.

A-Line: The skirt follows the line of an 'A'. This silhouette has been used in dresses, coats and jackets.

Page 109

Trumpet/Tulip: This example has six gores, three in the front and three in the back. The gored panels fit from waist to hip then flare out to the hem creating a trumpet effect.

Gored with Godets: This skirt has eight gores. The 'godet' is a triangular piece of fabric set into a seam to create even more flare.

Broomstick: An ankle-length skirt made in a fine fabric to allow for the gathering, it hangs straight.

Bias Cut: This skirt is cut out with the pattern pieces lying at forty-five degrees to the warp and weft, that is on the cross. Woven fabric has slightly stretchy properties at this angle and so allows for a better fit. Note that bindings are made from strips of fabric cut on the bias because they are much easier to manipulate around slight curves.

Wrap-over/Surplice: A common description for a garment that wraps across the front reaching the side seam and fastening at the waist.

Bubble/Haremor: Based on Turkish trousers, the skirt has a band at the hem which restricts movement.

Jeans Styling: The denim jean has influenced this skirt by continuing the use of topstitched seams, the jeans pocket and fly-front fastening.

Barrel/Tourneau/Pegged: This skirt is full at the top and tapered at the hem. The fullness at the waist is controlled by pleats, evenly distributed at either side of the centre front and held by the waistband.

Dirndl: A rectangle of fabric gathered up and held with a waistband, this is similar to the broomstick. There is no shaping.

Cheongsam: Of Chinese origin, this is a long, tight skirt that is slit almost to the waist at one or both sides.

Puff Ball: A similar approach to the dirndl except that here the fabric is folded in half and both edges are held by the waistband, thereby the fold in the fabric becoming the hem.

Page 110

Drape and Wrap-over: This skirt uses drape control by pleating and holding at the waistband. There is a wrapover for practicality.

Fishtail: A skirt that is shorter in the front than the back, often it is knee length in front and reaches the ground at the back, popular in the 1930s.

Handkerchief Hem: This skirt is cut as a large square with a hole in the centre. The waistband is attached to the hole in the centre consequently the square's corners hang in points.

Pareo: A rectangular piece of fabric wrapped around the body and tied in a knot, often with an exotic print or pattern. It is of Polynesian origin.

Wrap Tennis: A short, full skirt suspended from a yoke with a waistband and a slight wrap-over. For wear during tennis and other such like sports.

Fitted with Frill: A fitted skirt with a gathered frill attached to the hem.

Ire/Iro: A straight piece of printed cotton draped and pinned in place forming an over-tunic, it is worn by Nigerian women.

Yoke and Gathers: This example is indicated in a slightly stretchy fabric and would have overlocked edges. The skirt is made up of a yoke and gathered body.

Sarong: Similar to the pareo but much longer, this skirt consists of fabric about four, or so, metres long, sewn together at both ends to form a large tube. This is wrapped around the hips and tucked into a sash.

Petal: A skirt cut in shaped layers to resemble the petals of a flower.

Ra-Ra: A jersey fabric skirt, similar to the yoke and gathers skirt. Here the skirt body is split into two tiers. The use of a knitted fabric is indicated by the overlocked edges.

Tiered with Ruffles: The three tiers are separate and hang from the waistband. There are no gathers just circular cut ruffles, consequently lots of fullness and flare is achieved.

Peplum: This is a straight skirt with the peplum held in the waistband along with the base of the skirt. See **peplum jacket** for another variation.

Page 111

Feile Mor: In the seventeenth century, in Scotland, the tunic or shirt was superseded by the 'belted plaid' or feile mor. This consisted of a six-yard (5.5 m) length of cloth folded lengthways into pleats. The wearer then wrapped part of the fabric around his waist and fixed it with a belt, the remainder of the fabric was draped around the upper part of the body, fixed to one shoulder and allowed to fall down the back.

Inverted Box Pleat: This is the same as a box pleat but viewed from the other side, as the pleat would appear from the back. These pleats are permanent for the life of the garment in that they are permanently attached to the waistband, but the actual pleat itself may or may not be pressed, an unpressed pleat has a much rounder appearance.

Engineered Pleat: Here the pleats are placed wherever the designer wants them to appear. They can be asymmetrical and any type of pleat. This example shows the pleats topstitched to the hip.

Pleated Tennis Skirt: A sunray pleated short skirt, with a stripe running along the hem as a border. This skirt is used for tennis and other sports.

Skating Skirt: A very short sports skirt meant for skating, it has unpressed box pleats and is circular in cut. Generally worn with tights.

Fortuny Pleated: The name is derived from the Italian designer, Mario Fortuny, who created garments in silk that were permanently pleated. The pleats are quite fine and of a 'springy' nature because of the silk. Fortuny pleating has achieved cult status.

Crystal Pleated: Very fine pleats similar to knife pleats, these pleats are permanent for the life of the garment.

Filibeg/Kilt: A garment from the Scottish Highlands, the kilt is made in tartan with knife pleats and a self-fringe. The kilt pin is always an accessory for holding the wrap in place. See also **sporran and belt**.

Tiered: In this example contrasting fabrics draw attention to the tiers. The top of each panel is gathered to fit the bottom of the next.

Fustanella (Two Versions): This is a full and stiffly pleated skirt of white cotton or linen worn by Greek men as part of a traditional uniform.

Sunray Pleated: Here the pleat gradually gets wider towards the hem of the garment. Each pleat is identical and is of a wedge shape. These pleats are permanently pressed for the life of the garment.

Prairie: This is an ethnic, western style of skirt with a tiered body hanging from a fitted yoke. The yoke has a button-through front.

Box Pleated: In this example the pleats are formed by inserting fabric. The skirt fabric is split and rectangular pieces of a contrasting material set into it. These are then folded evenly so that the original split meets edge to edge. The actual silhouette of the garment does not change until the wearer moves and then the pleat is visible.

Knife Pleated: The pleats are even in width all round the body of the skirt. These pleats are permanently pressed for the life of the garment.

Page 112

Bustle: This skirt is created by draping fabric, there are no artificial supports. The base of the skirt is a dirndl, the top a piece of cloth folded and draped.

Hula/Grass: A traditional Hawaiian skirt made from grass and worn by both sexes.

Balayeuse/Sweeper's: The skirt has an underskirt with a finely pleated border called a dust ruffle.

Polonaise: Popular in the eighteenth and nineteenth centuries, the skirt is pulled up on cords into decorative swags or festoons to reveal an underskirt made in the same fabric.

Tablier/Apron with Train: 'Tablier' is a French expression for 'apron'. The bustle skirts of the 1860s and 1870s were draped up towards the back. The overskirt was usually open at the front and draped back at the sides forming an apron.

Vertugado Skirt with Aro: The skirt is bell shaped and originates from Spain. Cane strips called 'aro/ are inserted at regular intervals to maintain the shape.

Swimwear
Page 113

Dress and Bloomers: An early twentieth century swimsuit made up of dress and bloomers, attempting to cover as much of the body as possible. Such a garment would usually be knitted (pre Lycra, fine jersey did not appear until 1920 when Coco Chanel introduced wool jersey).

Two Piece: The swimsuit consists of two pieces, a top and high-waisted trunks, made in wool and worn with a belt.

Boxer Shorts: Elasticated shorts with internal support for men.

One Piece: Made in knitted wool, this 'all-in-one' was also worn with a belt.

Bikini: The briefest of swimwear for women, shown here with lace ties.

Micro Bikini: The extreme bikini designed for Chanel in 1996, leaves little to the imagination.

Four Piece Combination Bikini: A variety of cuts of tops and bottoms – tankinis, to ensure that the customer gets the best choice for their shape and leisure aspirations.

Trunks: Elasticated swimming trunks, made in a Lycra™ content fabric.

Bloomer Suit: Not unlike the maillot except that the legs are full and controlled by elastic and not as highly cut.

Corset over Bloomers: Early twentieth century swimwear, consisting of a lace-up corset and bloomers with pleated trims.

One Piece/Maillot (US): 'Maillot' is a French expression used regularly in America and relates to the fitting swimsuit in a modern Lycra content fabric. With higher cut legs and scoop neckline, this example shows a **racing/athletic** back, see Necklines. The garment is also known as a one-piece swimsuit or bathing suit.

Ballerina Suit with Trunks: A striped swimsuit dating from 1910 with long legged shorts and short dress over the top, note the changing direction of the stripes.

Dresses
Page 114
Sack/Shift: A straight dress with no construction lines.

A-Line: A dress, coat, skirt or jacket silhouette which echoes the shape of an 'A'.

Strapless: A dress constructed to stay in place without the aid of shoulder straps.

Blouson (Dropped Waist): Two silhouettes in one. The blouson is a loose fitting garment attached to a band of some sort. The dropped waist speaks for itself and can be taken to extremes.

Tiered: The silhouette is made up of a series of tiers. The tiers may be constructed from the same point, each subsequent tier being longer than the ones before, or the tiers may be attached to the garment at intervals.

Tent: This is similar to the trapeze silhouette but with a fuller flared skirt.

Trapeze: The silhouette is that of the trapezium, the shoulder and the hem being the parallel sides.

Dropped Waist: See **Blouson (dropped waist)**.

Sheath: A close fitting silhouette using darts.

Page 115
Empire Line: Inspired by Josephine, the French Empress at the beginning of the nineteenth century, this silhouette brought the waistline up under the bust with a gathered skirt. The skirt would hang straight, without any flare.

Shoulder Yoke: The sleeves and the body hang from the yoke.

Fit and Flare: Here the waistline is at normal level (the level can be moved up or down). The bodice fits and the skirt flares out.

Bouffant: A fitted bodice with full gathered skirt emphasising the roundness of the skirt.

Smock: A yoked shirt which was originally decorated with smocking – not necessarily so nowadays, but still retaining the name. It is often worn for maternity wear or as a coverall.

Princess Line: The construction line of this dress is close fitting to the waist, full and flaring below. Three panels in the front and three in the back are created by continuing the line of the darts all through the garment.

Cheongsam: A dress of Chinese origin, with deep slits up the side and a mandarin collar.

Page 116
Shirt: This is an extension of the shirt to a dress length, possibly with side slits. This example shows the placket fastening finishing just below the waist.

Wrap over/Surplice: A common word for the fastening of a garment which wraps across the front reaching the side seam at the waist line.

Coat: This dress looks and is constructed like a coat, but is more fitted to the body. It is frequently double breasted.

Shirt Waister: A waisted shirt extended to dress length, here with a full skirt and button-through placket front.

Cocktail: The early evening alternative to the ball gown, the cocktail dress is not quite as formal with the shorter length. This example is one interpretation, obviously dictated by fashion.

Fishtail/Mumu (US): This dress has a fitted body ending in a full skirt at calf length creating the impression of a fish tail. The American expression is a 'mumu', derived from a Hawaiian cotton wrapper.

Page 117

Tabard: A sleeveless tunic pulled on over the head and open at the sides, related to the Mandilion jacket. See also entry under Waistcoats.

Overall: Similar to the pinafore, but this garment can be pulled over the head. It may be made in a stretch fabric. It is known as a 'jumper' in America.

Tunic: A garment worn over a skirt or trousers, generally shorter than a normal dress length and which may or may not have sleeves.

Pinafore: A sleeveless dress usually with some form of fastening to be worn over a shirt or blouse.

Huipil: Worn with a straight skirt, the huipil was a loose, sleeveless blouse or dress cut straight, with holes for the head and arms. It was worn by the Mayan peasant.

Sarafan: A Slav woman's garment, the Sarafan has shoulder straps and is very full, almost circular. It is worn over a blouse and with a veil.

Page 118

Ballgown: The example given is just one way to interpret a ballgown as dictated by fashion. Often ballgowns are elaborate garments either in rich fabrics or ornate in detail, generally full length.

Tutu: A ballerina's dress with fitted bodice and multi-layered stiff net skirt giving an extreme silhouette.

Ballerina: An informal but dressy look of the post war years, this example has a stretch top, probably with Lycra™ content, giving a body hugging fit without darts.

Tee Shirt Dress: As the tee shirt this dress is made from a light jersey knitted fabric with a ribbed collar. Normally it is longer than the tee shirt and may have slits up the sides but it fits just as loosely.

Cotehardie: A tunic worn by both men and women from the late twelfth to the fourteenth century. See also man's example under Coats.

Flapper: A shift shaped dress with beaded trim associated with the 'flapper' of 1920s America, so called because she wore galoshes in the winter which were always unbuckled and flapping about.

Page 119

Prairie: An ethnic, Western style dress, with a full sleeve head and fitted bodice with placket forming a 'V' at the dropped waist. The skirt is tiered.

Peasant: A soft, full silhouette with an off-the-shoulder neckline and ethnic lace-up belt.

Dashiki: An ethnic garment similar to the caftan, with slightly more flared sleeves and ornamentation.

Indian Kurta: The kurta is a long blouse/dress, hanging to the knees, heavily decorated with gold embroidery.

Caftan: A long, ethnic, coat-like garment with long sleeves originating from the eastern coast of the Mediterranean.

Page 120

1940s Pannier Dress: This dress required a slender figure due to its panniers, gathers, pleats and ruching. Made in gold lamé it produced a fine sculpted effect.

Post War Dress: A variation of the shirt-waister style of dress, manufactured in a linen and cotton mix, which means it was hard wearing and fairly crease resistant.

1960s Knitted Dress: This dress was manufactured in gold lurex flecked yarn and has a typical 1960s appeal.

Prom Dress: This dress would be worn by young girls at formal dances, or proms (promenades). The prom was attended by American High School students. The dress would be worn with white gloves.

1950s Floral Print Dress: All-over prints were typical of the 1950s, especially in full-skirted dresses such as these.

Page 121

Leg of Mutton Dress: Highly decorated dress, worn at the beginning of the twentieth century, with bow features. The full sleeves helped to exaggerate the tiny waist.

Edwardian Dress with Train: This velvet dress has a low décolleté and long train. The style is that set by the 'Gaiety Girls' – actresses and singers popular at the time.

1950s Crinoline Dress: Synthetic fabrics allowed for new directions in fashion, here, the crinoline was resurrected, in nylon net over taffeta skirts and petticoats. The skirt's shape was achieved by the use of four stiff hoops and allowed the dress to stand unaided.

Page 122

Bliaud: See also man's **bliaud**. Women wore a ground-length bliaud, fitting more closely than the man's over the breasts and waist and having wide, open sleeves. They were highly decorated at the neck, waist and sleeve edge.

Sacque/Sac Dress: Loose pleats or folds fall from the shoulders of this garment to the floor. The front bodice is usually fitted to the waist and has a fine underskirt. It was popular in the sixteenth to eighteenth century.

Page 123

Houppeland with Dagges: A tunic worn by men and women in the fifteenth century, it was a long and voluminous gown with long hanging sleeves and a high, belted waist, usually made from a richly embroidered fabric and lined with fur. This example also shows dagges at the neckline and the sleeve edge. Dagges were an ornamental finish to the edge of fabric which was cut or serrated in a variety of patterns. See Production – Finishes.

Outdoor Dress: This dress originates from Basle in the fourteenth and fifteenth centuries. It consists of a full skirt and highly cut, fitted bodice. It has a very scooped neckline and fitted sleeve with a small puff. As the name suggests it was worn as outdoor dress.

Page 124

Toga: The toga originates in Ancient Rome and was a simple garment developing later into a large piece of fabric, about three times the height of its wearer, which was draped around the body in similar fashion to the himation. An abundance of folds was produced when the fabric was draped, one end was allowed to hang down the front over the left shoulder. The East African dur is very similar.

Peplos: A tunic arranged in folds which fastens in a drape with brooches at the shoulders. It originates from Ancient Greece and was worn by men and women.

Himation: A costume of the Ancient Greeks which consisted of a length of fabric draped around the body. This was a rectangular piece of cloth, with one end pulled from the back over the left shoulder, the rest of the fabric was pulled around the right side of the body and carried across the chest. The Abyssinian sharma is similar.

Chiton: A woman's garment from Ancient Greece, which was the peplos but with one shoulder bared.

Sari: A piece of cloth worn by women which is about 6.5 yards (6 m) long and a yard (1 m) wide and worn over a short blouse and a petticoat tied with a drawstring. The sari is tucked into the drawstring, loosely pleated and wrapped around the waist. The end (which can be very richly decorated) is carried over the left shoulder in the front and can be left to hang or be draped as a hood.

Page 125

Surcoat/Surcote: From 1340 until around 1460 the sideless surcoat was popular. The gown had a wide neckline and deep armholes, reaching to the hips. The neck and armholes would be finished with a band of fur or jewelled embroidery. See also Waistcoats – **surcoat**. This example is a later surcoat for men.

Dalmatica with Clavi: A loose garment worn by the Romans from around AD 190. It was made from Dalmatian wool (hence the name) and had long, wide sleeves. It was not belted. It was decorated by stripes of colour called 'clavi'.

Simlah with Tsitsith over Kethoneth: A Hebrew mantle with tassles over a tunic. The 'kenoneth' could be knee or ankle length, with short or long sleeves. The 'simlah' was generally a rectangle of fabric like the peplos. The 'tsitsith', or tassels, were an essential part of the decoration of Assyrian, Babylonian and Syrian dress.

Cassock: This gown is often made of wool and is trimmed with fur. It is narrower in cut than the houppeland and it is known as the cassock. There is a narrow opening for the head and a slit up the front, it finishes just above the shoes. It is worn with a leather belt, with purse, at hip level. This example is medieval, but the use of the term, with some modification of style, has continued to the present day as dress for the clergy.

Page 126

Angarka: Originating from Northern India, the angarka is usually made from muslin, but also calico, silk or wool, depending on the climate. The armpit is cut away and the garment wraps from side to side tying at the right side.

Bliaud: The bliaud was of Norman origin. The masculine version had a skirt of pleats and the sleeves widened into deep hanging cuffs. See also the woman's version in Dresses – woman's **bliaud**.

Yelek/Caftan: From the Near East, this is a woman's caftan buttoned to the waist and made from calico. It could also be silk or brocade.

Page 127

Mashlah: A garment that originates from Nazareth, it is elongated and very simple in cut, made from cotton and embroidered in a variety of silks.

Jibbah/Jubbah: Known as the jubbah by Turks and the jibbah by Egyptians, this is an unlined garment of any colour of cloth. It is flared and seamed to add the extra width.

Shirts
Page 128

Lumberjack/Logger's: A heavy, warm, woollen shirt made in mackinaw fabric. See **mackinaw cruiser**.

Polo Shirt: See Knitwear – **polo shirt**.

Formal/Dress: The same style as the man's shirt except that the formal shirt has a wing collar and tucked front and is traditionally white.

Cycling Jersey: An extra long top made in breathable fabric that wicks away moisture while cycling, usually decorated by stripings.

Fisherman's Smock: A simple fisherman's work shirt with bateau collar and large patch pockets.

Garibaldi Blouse/Shirt: This shirt or blouse was inspired by the visit to Britain of Giuseppe Garibaldi in 1863 and the famous 'Red shirts' which were worn by his small army. The shirt was made from red wool decorated with black braid and had full sleeves, gathered into a fitted cuff.

Western: Of American origin and commonly related to Country and Western music, this shirt was originally worn by cowboys. The 'V' yokes and patch breast pocket are hallmarks, especially when braided.

Work: A simple shirt with a placket fastening that ends just above the waist, it has a mandarin collar.

Parachute Shirt: Designed by Vivienne Westwood for sale at 'Sex' in 1976. This shirt employed the 'bondage' ethic of multiple straps, an essential part of the punk look. Bondage dressing was based on the straitjacket.

Page 129

Henley: A woven fabric shirt, the same silhouette as the tee shirt, with a button placket and crew neck.

Steelmaker's: A simple work shirt in knitted jersey similar to the tee shirt.

Cossack: An ethnic tunic-like top with asymmetrical fastening and a straight band collar.

Man's: The loose garment worn by men and boys under a waistcoat and jacket, usually with a yoke, button placket, shirt collar and inverted box pleat in the back.

Tee Shirt: A classic cult pull-on top, the tee shirt is made in fine jersey fabric with a knitted rib, crew neckline and is derived from underwear.

Bowling: A loose fitting shirt with short sleeves and patch breast pocket worn for ten pin bowling and normally having team names embroidered on the back and the pocket. Of American origin.

Evening Shirt with Chitterlings: Chitterlings are the lace or linen frills worn on the front of a man's shirt from the late eighteenth to the nineteenth century. They are now usually used for evening wear, as here on an evening shirt.

Sailor: A loose shirt borrowed from the American and British Navy, having the sailor collar, broad and square in the back and narrowing in the front. See **sailor collar**.

Tops
Page 130

Shell Blouse: A simple, sleeveless, slightly loose blouse.

Princess: Darts are continued through the body of the garment forming separate panels and construction lines.

Normal Fitted: As the shell blouse, a very simple, sleeveless but fitted blouse.

Overblouse: A straight-cut top worn over shirts and blouses.

Blouson on Yoke: A deep yoke band supporting a full blouson top with bateau neckline.

Ballerina/Dance: A jersey/knitted top with wrapover fronts. The ties wrap around the back and tie in the front.

Shoulder Yoke: The body of the top hangs from the square yoke.

Bandeau: A narrow band of fabric covering the bust. This example shows the band simply knotted in front, it is ideal for beachwear.

Strapless: A short, fitted top that has no straps for support, but relies on the fit of the garment.

Bustier: A sleeveless, fitted top, usually ending just above the hips. It is meant to emphasise the bust. This example has a halter neck, that is, the support straps wrap around the neck rather than over the shoulders.

Surplice/Wrap-over: A wrap-over blouse where the fronts wrap over and under to the opposite side seam and fasten at the waist.

Camisole: Originally a sleeveless under-bodice, worn over stays or corsets to protect the dress. More recently it has become a simple cotton top, often decorated with lace or broderie anglais.

Boob Tube: A tube of stretch fabric, that covers the bust.

Peasant Blouse: There are two examples here. The peasant blouse is a generic term. One of the blouses is off the shoulder, with a deep feminine frill, elasticated for a body hugging fit at the waist. The other also has an elasticated neck (in a deep scoop) and waist, and full elasticated sleeves.

Smock: A yoked shirt with full sleeves and body. See **smock dress**.

Petenlair: A style of short jacket, designed with a sacque back and worn with a petticoat. It originated in France in the mid eighteenth century. The skirt was made from the same fabric and later adopted the same term.

Casaquin: Similar in description to the petenlair, but much lighter in weight. Again it is meant to be made in the same fabric as the skirt so that it looks like a one piece garment and has the sacque back.

Page 131

Choli: A woman's bodice from Northern India, which fastens at the back and is heavily decorated with braid.

Moravian Blouse: A short, but full, woman's blouse cut in the Slavian fashion. It has a deep collar decorated with braid, as are the full sleeves.

Mandarin: A fitted Chinese top with an asymmetrical fastening and mandarin collar which has short sleeves and side slits. It is made in a woven fabric, originally silk.

Singlet: A man's vest originally, now often worn by girls as underwear and outerwear. The vest originally buttoned at the neck with a small button placket and tiny buttons.

Sports Tank: A slightly A-line top, that is sleeveless and has a low neckline. It is meant for athletic sports and made in a breathable fabric. It is usually colour blocked in some way.

Middy Blouse (US): A feminine version of the sailor influence, this top has the obligatory sailor collar and an elasticated waist. It is known as the 'middy' because it was based upon the midshipman's navy and white top. It was popular around the 1930s.

Mandarin Work Top: Practical Chinese work wear, usually cotton and of simple construction.

Page 132

Ssitar: This garment originates from Kurdistan and is a short shirt made from twill. The long, pointed sleeves are wound around the wrists or tied in a knot behind the neck. It has gussets under the arms for extra movement and 'lift'.

Doublet with Counterchange Design: A fourteenth-century patterned top. The pattern shows a motif in two colours in one part of the design with the colours reversed in the other. This was very fashionable in parti-coloured garments. See also Suits – **parti-coloured dress and harlot**.

Djellabah: An outer garment from North Africa, made from coarse woollen or cotton fabric. This example is hooded and very square in cut with large gussets under the arm.

Buff Coat: A tan-coloured soft leather top, with a contrasting falling band and sash.

Kimono: A loose Japanese top, wrapped and tied with an **obi**, see **Belts**. Traditionally worn by men and women fastened from left to right, here the kimono is tied in the western woman's way.

Page 133

Giaberello: From the Italian Renaissance, the fourteenth and fifteenth centuries, this garment is constructed from semi-circular pieces of fabric sewn together at the centre to form flat pleats. The fabric is often rich brocade and the garment is frequently fur trimmed.

Doublet: A basic upper garment, sleeved or sleeveless, for men, usually shaped to fit the body (with or without padding depending on the period). It was worn, in one form or another from medieval times until the first half of the seventeenth century.

Cotehardie: Worn from the twelfth to the fourteenth century, this is a close-fitting tunic-like top falling to the hip for men and the ground for women.

Slashed Doublet: See Trousers – **trunk hose (slashed)** for a full explanation of slashing.

Peasecod Bellied Doublet: A doublet that was popular in the 1580s, which gave a protuberant stomach silhouette, this was achieved by padding the front of the doublet into an artificial paunch which was maintained by a wooden busk at the front and whalebone strips in the seams. This is a side view.

Pagliaccio/Pierrot: A shirt derived from the Italian stage comedy character, popular in the second half of the sixteenth century. He appeared in French comedy as Pierrot and the English version is the clown. These characters wore loose white clothes with a deep ruffle at the neck and large buttons. The shirt sleeves and body are very flared and full.

Gipon/Gambeson: A Christian warrior's, tight, long-sleeved, parti-coloured doublet. The metal girdle is worn slung low on the hips.

Loungewear
Page 134

NB The loungewear garments are rather antiquated – no longer do we lounge around like we used to!

Boudoir Jacket: A jacket for lounging, with puffed sleeves and lace collar, worn at the time when leisure activities were more limited to the upper classes who would relax and receive guests at their homes. This example dates from around the early part of the twentieth century.

Dressing Sacque: This short jacket is of the type worn in poorly heated bedrooms when dressing, which was a long process for the leisured classes in the eighteenth and nineteenth centuries.

Combing Jacket/Powdering Mantle/Peignoir: This coat was used for informal wear in the morning and, as the name suggests, for grooming.

Hostess Coat/House Coat: This was an informal lounge coat.

Negligée: This negligée is meant for lounging not for sleeping.

Page 135

Brocade Robe: A lounging coat made in rich fabrics.

Robe de Chambre: A dressing gown with a large soft collar and wrap-over front.

Hostess Pyjama: An easy and comfortable pyjama meant for lounging.

Page 136

Matinée Jacket: A lounging jacket that is sleeveless but quite full for comfort.

Morning Jacket: As the name suggests, a jacket worn for lounging in the morning, a term which, up to the mid-nineteenth century, covered the whole period before dinner (served between four and eight o'clock).

Kimono: This kimono shows the traditional shaped sleeves (which could be used as pockets) and wrapped front.

Lounging Pyjamas: These became popular during the 1920s evolving from trouser wearing which began when women worked in factories during World War I. These would be worn around the house during the day.

Nightwear
Page 137

Breakfast Cape/Bed Rayle: This garment was used to keep the shoulders warm whilst breakfasting in bed. It is a drawstring cape.

Bed Jacket: This garment has the same function as the bed rayle.

Boudoir Rayle: This garment was used in the bedroom and was placed over the shoulders whilst grooming the hair.

Baby Doll's: A tiny transparent nightdress with matching briefs for sleeping, very popular in the late 1960s.

Night Cloak/Travelling Cloak: This garment has the same function as the dressing gown.

Mandarin Sleepcoat: The Chinese version of sleepwear, note the typical asymmetrical fastening and mandarin collar.

Nightgown: This garment is now better known as a nightdress.

Page 138

Negligée (Bias Cut): Originally worn for lounging at home, nowadays the gown is worn for sleeping. This particular example shows a body-hugging gown in a woven fabric, but the garment was cut on the cross for an even slinkier fit. See also Skirts – **bias cut**.

Shortie Nightdress: The nightdress is short and has a drawstring neck.

Bath Robe: A short, mid-thigh length gown for use after bathing and also as a dressing gown, it is made from towelling.

Knitted Pyjamas: British Colonials copied pyjamas from India and Persia around 1870. Originally for loungewear they eventually usurped the nightshirt. This example is knitted for warmth and comfort and has snug fitting ribbed cuffs.

Striped Pyjamas: The traditional pyjama with breast pocket and either elasticated or drawstring waist to the bottoms. See also **knitted pyjamas**.

Page 139

Sleepsuit (All-in-One): This is an extension of the traditional pyjama. Here the stripes run the full length of the body.

Nightshirt: The nightshirt was used before pyjamas were discovered, it was like an exaggerated shirt with a shirt hem but reaching the ankles.

Dressing Gown: A traditional type of dressing gown with satin collar, patterned body and rope belt.

Sleepcoat: This garment is tied with a self-belt and sometimes worn instead of pyjamas.

Loose Cut Pyjamas: These pyjamas were made from artificial silk jersey and date from 1930s.

Women did not begin to wear pyjamas until the 1920s.

Knitwear
Page 140

Tee Shirt: A classic cult pull-on top, the tee shirt is made in fine jersey fabric with a knitted rib, crew neckline and is derived from underwear.

Army Sweater: A knitted, ribbed sweater, usually olive drab in colour, it has reinforcing patches of cotton fabric on the shoulders and elbows. Worn generally by the armed forces, the air force have a similar garment normally blue in colour.

Grandad Shirt: A jersey fabric shirt, collarless, but with a short button placket, small buttons and long fitted sleeves.

Polo Shirt: A knitted cotton fabric pull-on shirt with a ribbed collar and cuffs. There is often a stripe running through the collar and cuffs and a short button placket.

Crew Neck Pullover/Sloppy Joe (Fully Fashioned): The term 'fully fashioned' is applied to garment construction using modern machine knitted pieces that are designed for socks, sweaters, thick tights, cardigans etc., where the flat sections are shaped by adjusting the number of stitches to fashion the garment pieces which are later seamed together. Here the sweater is shaped at the raglan sleeve. This is the more costly alternative to using jersey knit fabric, the more usual process for underwear, tee shirts etc (see **cut and sew sweatshirt**).

Guernsey: A traditional fisherman's sweater from the Channel Islands knitted in heavy wools where the natural oils are retained to make the garment warm and water repellent, normally a dark navy in colour. Very similar in philosophy to the **Aran sweater**.

Cut and Sew Sweatshirt: 'Cut and sew' is the description of the method of making a garment from knitted fabric. The garment pieces are cut out from the fabric which is laid out as if it was a woven fabric, with pattern pieces placed upon it, and then sewn together as normal. Different stitches and finishes have to be used to maintain the natural stretch of the fabric.

Cricket Sweater: Worn traditionally by cricketers, the sweater is always white or cream, with coloured stripes around the neck band and hem ribbing. There may also be cabling repeated all over the garment.

Punk String Knit: These garments had a very unstructured, distressed look, and could be knitted in mohair or string/net. The mohair version was available at 'Sex' in the Kings Road in 1976. The net/string top was available at 'Seditionaries' in 1977 (Seditionaries was the follow up to Sex at the same location in the Kings Road and the designer was Vivienne Westwood.)

Rugby Shirt: A sports shirt with a knitted collar and long sleeves with knitted cuffs. The hallmark of the rugby shirt is the brightly coloured stripes running horizontally across the body.

Vest: A scooped neck and armholes form the vest which is made in stretch jersey fabric so that it can be pulled over the head without the need for fastenings.

Page 141

Intarsia knit: Intarsia is a knit stitch where colour changes are introduced into a garment and the yarns twisted to prevent holes appearing. Colour changes can be as frequent as desired by the designer.

Fair Isle Sweater/Jacquard: Supposedly originating from Fair Isle, but quite widespread in Scotland. Fair Isle knitting consists of colourful stripings of geometric symbols and shapes on the front of the garment, a similar effect to a jacquard pattern. Across the back are floaters where the yarns are carried across when a colour changes. The traditional patterns are such that on any one row only two colours are used.

Boob Tube: A tube of stretch knitted fabric that covers the bust and waist.

1950s Embroidered Cardigan: The 1950s were a fun fashion period including the demand for fancy knitwear. The development of new manufacturing techniques allowed for mass produced items in elaborate designs at reasonable cost.

1940s Jumper: Various textures and thicknesses of yarn, unpicked from old garments, due to the war effort, resulted in this type of sweater, very often with short sleeves and the high waist.

1950s Beaded Cardigan: Heavily beaded and embroidered cardigans were worn as evening wear in the 1950s and were later much sought after in the early 1980s as vintage wear.

Skinny Rib: A ribbed sweater that hugs the body.

Twin Set: A sweater and cardigan knitted in the same colour and yarn and with the same stitch so that they can be worn together. Occasionally the sweater would be knitted without sleeves.

Aran Sweater: Originating as fishermen's garments from the Aran Islands off the west coast of Ireland, these are knitted in heavy natural wool retaining the water repellent natural oils. The Aran sweater combines numerous stitches, such as cables, knots and ribs. The sweaters were traditionally knitted slightly differently so that fisherman lost at sea could be identified when washed up on shore.

Tank Top: A sleeveless top, less formal than a waistcoat, worn over shirts and with skirts or trousers. This example has deep waist, armhole and V-neck ribbing. The body of the garment may be heavily patterned.

Cardigan: A knitted garment with ribbing trims and a button-through front fastening. It originated from the Earl of Cardigan, a General in the Crimean War, who wore a short military jacket of knitted worsted.

Underwear
Page 142
Bandalette: A very brief arrangement of crossover ties.

Bra (Wrap-over): A bra that has no shaping and so gives the effect of flattening the breasts for the silhouette popular in the 1920s. It is made from strong white cotton covering the body to the waist with shoulder support straps.

Flattener Brassiere: This brassiere provided little support but did help to restrict the bust to the desired shape that was popular in the 1920s. Similar to the wrap-over bra.

Bosom Amplifier: As the name suggests, this garment exaggerates the size of the breasts using the soft layering of lace to give the shape fashionable in the first decade of the twentieth century.

Balconette Bra: A cut-away bra that reveals more of the cleavage.

Sports Bra: A stretch fabric bra that gives support during sporting activity, often with a racing back as here.

Strapless Bra: A bra that is constructed to support the breasts without relying on straps.

Apodesme: An ancient Greek garment that is made of a band of wool or linen wrapped across the breasts and tied or pinned into place.

Underwired Bra: Wire is incorporated in the cup of the bra to give extra support and uplift.

Wonderbra™/Uplift Bra: A bra designed specifically to enhance the size and shape of the breasts.

Fifties Uplift: This bra is constructed by many rows of circular stitching which causes the bra cup to point upwards and outwards and so gives support and shape.

Bustier: A fitted bra which also covers the waistline and sometimes goes over the hips, it can be made in daywear fabrics and worn as a top. See also Tops – **bustier.**

Backless Bra: This is a simple cover-up fastened with ties.

Basque: This is a term for the extension of the corset below the waist, often trimmed with lace.

Gourgandine: This is a soft corset with no boning for support.

Suspender Belt: This is a Utility suspender belt and so is quite a bit plainer than would be expected. Utility clothing followed a strict code of practice which meant using less fabric, and fewer trimmings and fastenings.

The trade mark was 'CC41' for 'civilian clothing introduced in 1941' and enduring in production until 1951.

Merry Widow: A type of corselette that fits tightly over the top of the hips, waist and rib cage, with half cups that push the bust upwards. An hour-glass silhouette is achieved. With the corset being short this necessitates the suspenders being long. The garment was named after Lehar's operetta, The Merry Widow. It is also worn with can-can dresses.

Longline Bra: Cut as an ordinary bra but with a longer body, usually to the waist.

Page 143
Planchette: A French expression for a padded corset. Note the direction of the striped fabric.

Corset/Stays: Corset is a French expression and usurped stays, the garment was meant to emphasise the natural body shape.

Corps de Fer: An iron corset covered in fabric.

Corps Pique: A quilted corset.

Basquine: Not unlike the basque, but the bust is not so defined.

Corselette: A lighter weight version of the corset.

Corselette (Half Bra): As the corselette, but here with a half-cut bra to reveal more of the cleavage and breast.

Zona: A soft, shaped, wide, body-hugging belt made in leather.

Echelle: A stomacher, trimmed down the front with ribbons which reduce in scale towards the bottom of the panel.

Stomacher: A long, ornate panel forming the front of a bodice.

Guepiere/Waist Cincher: As the names suggest, a fitted, laced garment meant to give a wasp-like waist.

Spoon Busk/Swan Bill Busk/Pear Shaped Busk: The busk is the stiffener in the stays and is normally a piece of whalebone or wood. As the names suggest these come in a variety of shapes.

Pregnancy/Nursing Corset: Here there are laced areas to allow for an expanding abdomen and breasts and for breastfeeding the child after birth. Nowadays, of course, although good support is advised for the expanding breasts, there are usually no restrictions on the abdomen and modern nursing bras have a zip or stud fastening for easy one-handed access.

Waspie: The corset designed to maintain Dior's 'New Look' in the late 1940s.

Foundation Garments: Two variations of a fitted combination of bra and girdle, occasionally with boning to create a particular shape. A 1960s firm control garment, the antithesis of the desires of the women's liberation movement, more reminiscent of the 1950s and usurped by the girdle made in Lycra™ and Spandex™.

Page 144

Vest: An undergarment worn next to the skin and often made of merino wool, or a jersey fabric.

String Vest: Popular in the 1950s and 1960s. The mesh is made from a string-like yarn and is very open.

Thermal Vest: Thermal fabrics trap air in tiny pockets and so aid in retaining warmth. Thermals have been around for a long time, but became fashionable in the 1980s. The best known thermal underwear manufacturer was Damart.

Girdle with Suspenders: A body-hugging, shaping garment made in a stretch fabric, with suspenders attached for wearing stockings.

Leotard: Traditionally black and always with long sleeves, the leotard was designed by Jules Leotard, a nineteenth-century trapeze artist. The garment is worn for dancing and gymnastics and is always made in a stretch fabric.

Thong Brief/Aerobics Brief: A cut-away, high-leg brief worn during exercise, usually with tights.

Bodyshaper: A fitting body made from a firm fabric and with a press-stud crutch.

Teddy: An all-in-one body combining slip and knickers, with a press-stud crutch.

G-String: A very brief brief used, for example, by fashion models because it is easy to conceal. It is made in a stretch fabric. This is a back view and shows the very fine 'string' at the back.

Briefs: Small knickers made in a stretch fabric.

French Knickers/Cami-knickers: Full, soft knickers, often made in silk for luxury and comfort.

Combinaire: This garment was made from artificial silk jersey with elastic suspenders. It was designed to flatten curves during the 1920s.

Pantie Girdle: A body forming, stretch garment, in the form of pants and with suspenders attached.

Thermals: Long-legged underwear worn specifically for warmth. The warmth comes from the specialist fabric designed to retain heat. See **thermal vest**.

Y-Fronts: Underpants worn by men and made in a stretch fabric.

Loincloth: A very brief garment of the Far and Middle East made up of a piece of fabric wrapped around the loins.

Underdrawers: Made of linen and always white.

Peasant Drawers: A very brief version of drawers worn in medieval times.

Boxer Shorts: Elasticated shorts with internal support for men, made in woven fabrics.

Knickerbocker Bloomer: As knickerbockers but baggier and meant as underwear. They are elasticated at the waist and hem.

Page 145

Drawstring Drawers: A linen undergarment drawn up with drawstrings at the waist and hem.

Umbrella Drawers: Flaring drawers with no gathers, decorated with lace and bows.

Knickerbockers: Like **knickerbockers** in Trousers, but here meant as underwear and trimmed with lace. They are cut without a crutch seam, hence the fullness in that area.

Opera Drawers: Like drawers but open at the back, 'opera' meaning an opening.

French Drawers: A full knicker with no drawing in at the hem, worn under full skirts.

Dance Set: A matching bra and knickers set, popular in the middle of the twentieth century.

Camesia: An undergarment or sleeping garment from Greece.

Directoire Knickers: The name is derived from similar pantaloons worn by French ladies in Paris during the Directory rule at the end of the eighteenth century. An essential garment for wearers who enjoyed high kicking dances such as the Blackbottom and Charleston.

Brassiere: This brassiere provided little support but did help to restrict the bust to the desired shape that was popular in the 1920s.

Envelope Chemise: A chemise and drawers combined.

Chemiset: A short linen undergarment.

Chemise Slip: A short all-in-one undergarment (top and skirt combined).

Combination Corset Cover and Knickerbockers: This garment is worn over the corset. It has a button-through front and the legs are drawn in.

Page 146

Gored Petticoat with Dust Ruffles: A full-length underskirt with a tier of ruffles that are meant to protect the overdress from dust.

Half Slip: An underskirt without a top, fitting at the waist, shown here with finely pleated tiers.

Bustle Petticoat with Button-on Underskirt: A smooth fronted underskirt with tiered frills buttoning onto the back of the garment at the sides.

Bustle Petticoat: A full underskirt with a drawstring back worn over a bustle. This is a side view.

Petticoat (Boned): A boned, elasticated waistband supports a full skirt and helps to create the desired silhouette.

Page 147

Bodystocking: An all-in-one, full body with feet. It is always made in a stretch fabric and can be pulled on.

Union Suit/Combinations/Long Johns: An all-in-one man's undergarment worn for warmth in cold climates, or for winter sporting activities.

Footless Tights/Leggings: More recently known as leggings, these are not really underwear as such, but they can be worn under tunics, dresses and skirts. See also Trousers – **leggings**.

Drawers (Separate Legs): Two legs of hose, with feet, held together at the waist with ties.

Pantalettes: Worn by younger girls in the mid-nineteenth century and falling below the skirt or dress hemline.

Long Johns: This garment is the bottom half only of the combinations but has the same function. It is made of a ribbed fabric with finer ribbed cuffs at the ankle.

Princess Slip: A full underskirt following the princess line of construction (i.e. a series of seams following the line of the darts right through the garment from shoulder to hem and creating panels). This example shows a deep skirt border which stops the panelling around the thigh.

Page 148

Ski Underwear: A sweat top and bottoms worn for warmth when skiing, usually bright red in colour.

Tobe: An Arabian undergarment, made in cotton and reaching ankle length, worn under an aba. See Outerwear – **aba/abayeh**.

Stola: An under-tunic of ancient Greece, reaching the ankle, long and straight in silhouette, but with a pleated front and drawstring waist.

Bustle (Spiral Wire): This example is made from a flexible spiral of wire.

Crinoline Hoop (Steel): This steel crinoline is supported by braces.

Plastic Frame Crinoline: A modern interpretation of the crinoline, plastic being quite a lot lighter than metal.

Page 149

Panniers (Metal): These fold up for storage and are fitted using the tapes around the waist.

Pleated Crinoline Wheel: This crinoline in very stiff fabric is tied onto the body at the waist helping to form a bell type silhouette.

Farthingale Bolster/Waist Bolster/Bum Barrel: A bolster that was tied around the waist to form a full silhouette, emphasising the body just above the hips.

Janseniste Panniers: This garment is made up of panniers with gaps for using the pockets in an undergarment.

Bustle Crinoline: Here the silhouette is preformed with the emphasis on the back, creating the interesting but exaggerated side view fashionable around 1900.

Bustle Cushion: One or more cushions filled with cork or light stuffing and tied around the waist.

Sleeve Cushions: The same principle as the bustle cushion but here to create puffed sleeves.

Criade: The criade is a skirt support made of gummed canvas or oilcloth and wire.

Wheel Farthingale: A skirt supported by hoops of whalebone or wire to maintain the wheel shape.

ACCESSORIES

Bags
Page 150

Clutch Bag: This is like the envelope clutch but without the flap.

Pillow Bag: A large, soft, squashy bag – like a pillow.

Shoulder Bag (Top Handle): The carrying handle is attached to the sides at the mouth of the bag and supported on the wearer's shoulder.

Swagger Pouch: A firm framed handbag with double handles, one mounted on each side of the opening.

Envelope Clutch: There are no straps or handles for carrying this bag, it is carried in the hand and has a flat opening – the 'envelope'.

Chain/Chanel: A quilted bag with a flap and a chain carrier, designed by Coco Chanel.

Double Bag (Central Clasp): A central clasp splits the bag into two. It has a firm frame and is barrel shaped.

Basket Bag: A rounded, basket effect bag.

Bracelet Handle: This bag has rigid circular handles, like bracelets, possibly made of wood.

Sausage Bag: A long sausage-shaped bag with a single handle mounted on one side of the bag which is usually made from leather.

Evening Bag with Pantographic Fastener: A decorative bag which opens by means of a series of metal strips that work like an accordion.

Crescent Shaped Bag: A soft bag shaped as the name suggests.

Almoner Purse: Popular around the fourteenth century and later. The almoner was a bag for carrying money.

Evening Bag: Heavily beaded, contemporary, desirable evening bag, designed to add luxury to an outfit.

String Bag: A bag fabricated of a network of strong cord that expands as it is filled, usually with leather handles attached by metal rings, although it can be totally made of cord.

Feed Bag: A soft bag drawn up to fasten, reminiscent of a horse's feed-bag.

Reticule: Made from net mesh fabric and often used for evening wear, this example shows the net hanging from a bracelet handle. The net is pulled apart to open.

Mesh Evening Bag: This example would be made from silver mesh with an amethyst clasp, used early in the twentieth century.

Document Case: A flat case usually made of leather with a zip fastener which is designed to accommodate documents. It may or may not have a handle.

Tote Bag: A large double handled, easy to carry handbag.

Shoe Bag: As the name suggests, a bag for carrying a single pair of shoes.

Kelly Bag: A bag that was carried and made famous by Grace Kelly, the actress who became a princess by marrying Prince Rainier of Monaco.

Sally Jess Bag: A bag made of two pieces of fabric stitched together with a handle contrived from the fabric, as designed by Sally Jess in the 1960s.

Bandoleer/Pouch: Nomadic American Indians carried this bag on their shoulders containing their few possessions. It was made of dyed skins and highly embroidered, incorporating beads and quills.

Barrel Bag: A long rounded bag with wrap-around handles, here shown in one piece.

Carpet Bag: A full, fabric bag often with wooden handles forming part of the framework.

Page 151

Luggage Handle: A firm handle, preformed and usually seen on suitcases.

Hat Box: A firm oval box for carrying and protecting hats.

Wig Box: A rounded box with a zip half way down, used to carry wigs. The handle is a loop fixed in the centre of the top.

Muff: A tube of insulated fabric, often fur, which is used to keep the hands warm so there is access at both ends. There is a zip purse inside this muff for keeping small change.

Box Bag: Shaped like a box, with a flap for fastening and a firm sturdy handle.

Vanity Box: This bag is used for carrying cosmetics and usually includes a mirror in the lid. It is a firm-framed box.

Oxford Bag: A large, firm-framed bag covered with leather and with a rigid handle for strength.

Fishing Bag: A soft, canvas bag with leather straps to fasten over a flap. There is a mesh pocket on the front to hold oddly shaped items.

Duffle Bag: A deep bag made in many fabrics, usually reinforced at the top and bottom. The bag is closed by a drawstring through the eyeleted top. The drawstring is attached to the base of the bag and forms the handle, the bag being worn slung over the shoulder.

Bucket Bag: A large open-topped bag.

Ski Bag: A long, thin bag for carrying skis and poles. The handles wrap around the body of the bag for strength. There is a long zip fastener for easy access.

Lifestyle Bag: The 1990s brought 'lifestyle' to the consumer. This shiny, practical, bag allowed the owner to store all their modern accessories – mobile phone, credit cards as well as their usual effects.

Bum Bag: A recent development of the purse belt, the bag is crescent shaped and hung on a webbing clip belt worn slung around the waist. It may have multiple pockets and double zippers.

Rucksack: A large canvas bag with many compartments for carrying supplies. It is carried on the back with the straps hooked around the front of the arms, the weight being taken on the shoulders.

Courier Bag for Cycle: A bag that is attached to a bicycle for carrying supplies, documents etc. It has leather straps and handle.

Roll Holdall: A rounded, canvas holdall with webbing straps that wrap around the body of the bag.

Panniers: Two identical bags attached side by side, usually in leather or canvas. They are carried by the strap that joins them, or they are slung over a horse or motorcycle, the weight of their contents balancing on either side.

Sports Bag: A rigid framed canvas bag with webbing carrying handles and shoulder strap, meant for carrying sports equipment and clothing.

Page 152

Suit Case: A piece of luggage, not only for packing suits. This example has reinforced corners and studding for strength and decoration.

Shopping Bag: A large, simple shaped, strong bag with reinforced handles.

Doctor's Bag/Gladstone Bag: A traditional bag used by doctors, similar to the Oxford bag. Also made famous by Gladstone who carried a version.

Satchel: A bag used for carrying school books, very strong and usually made from leather. It is carried on the back or shoulder with adjustable straps.

Compact: A small, highly decorated flat box for holding compressed powder, usually metal sometimes plastic. There can be a mirror in the lid and the powder in the base topped off with a puff or sponge for application.

Cigarette Case: Cigarette cases are usually made of metal and contain strapping to hold the cigarettes in place and possibly a mirror. Not so popular nowadays, they were a common accessory in the first half of the twentieth century. They can be quite ornate and decorative and are often personalised.

Snuff Bottle: See **snuff box**. Snuff bottles were widely used in the Orient in the eighteenth and nineteenth centuries. Again these were intricately decorated and beautifully made.

Snuff Box: Snuff is a preparation of powdered tobacco, the inhaling of which become popular in Europe in the late seventeenth century and continued to be so, for both sexes, until early in the nineteenth century. Snuff boxes were devised to carry the powder in the pocket and could be intricately made and decorated.

Brief Case: Like the attaché case and document case, this bag is designed for carrying papers. It may be made from leather or any other durable fabric.

Attaché Case: A hand-carried case with a rigid frame designed for carrying papers. It is often made in metal covered in leather or other strong fabrication.

Evening Bag with Trousse: A bag with a vanity section, including mirror and cosmetics, as well as a purse section.

Necessaire Box: A zip fastening vanity case for men, including grooming equipment for nails and hair.

Collar Box: A rigid box for carrying and protecting detachable collars.

Top Hat Box: A rigid box for carrying non-collapsible top hats.

Portmanteau: This literally means a 'coat carrier'. It is a suitcase with a rigid handle.

Suit Bag: This bag opens out to allow suits to be laid in and fastened in place, with a zip covering. It folds for ease of carrying but can be hung up or laid flat open to minimise creasing.

Bellows Case: The case expands owing to the accordion effect pleating. The leather straps wrapped around the case offer support.

Steamer Trunk: A firm-framed piece of luggage, including drawers and coat hangers which acts as a mini wardrobe while travelling, especially by sea.

Gloves
Page 153

Seams
Out Seam: The reverse of in seams, the raw edges are seen on the outside of the glove, this does not present any problems when skins are used.

Over Seam: As the out seams but overstitched instead of flat locked.

Full Pique Seam: The cloth is wrapped under or over itself and stitched.

In Seam: The seams are tiny, but are like conventional flat-lock seams on the inside of the glove.

Half Pique Seam: Two of the seams are wrapped over, the other two are 'in seams'.

Thumbs
Set-in Thumb: Probably the most common thumb treatment.

French/Quirk: A gusset type of thumb treatment.

Novelty Thumb: The thumb is a separate piece of cloth set into the glove.

English: This is a complicated construction, which aids flexibility.

Styles
Fingerless: This is like a normal glove except that the tops have been removed. Often it is knitted but it is sometimes made of leather.

Fingerless Lace Mitten: This mitten has very short fingers and is for formal and special occasions.

Cycling Mitten: A fingerless mitten with leather palm and string back for cycling. It has a stretch rib cuff.

Decorated Mitten: This is a long glove with no fingers and half a thumb, highly decorated with gold threads on satin, for formal occasions.

Shooting: Used when shooting to protect the hand, it has an elasticated cuff.

Woodstock/Riding: A fawn skin glove used for horse riding.

Limerick: A glove made in newborn lamb leather.

Hawking: This fourteenth century glove was for hawking. It is long and made in leather to protect the arm.

York Tan: This can be a short or long glove named after its colour – tan.

Slip-on: There are no fastenings, the glove is just pulled on.

Sports Glove: An insulated leather glove used in outdoor sports.

Button Length/Mousquetaire: A long evening glove with a short wrist opening and small pearl buttons.

Glove with Liner: Two gloves in one for extra warmth.

Mitten: Four fingers are covered together, the thumb is solitary. This mitten can be knitted, woven or made from leather.

Gauntlet Mitten: A mitten with a protective forearm cuff.

Berlin: A thin and neat glove made in strong cotton.

Knitted: As the name suggests, a totally knitted glove with no need for a gusset.

Shortie: A wrist length glove, made in kid, cotton or nylon. It was very fashionable from the mid 1940s to the 1960s.

Gauntlet: A glove with a protective forearm cuff, this example shows the gauntlet cut in panels.

Golfing: Very similar to the driving glove, there are cut-outs over the knuckles and often a cut-out over the back of the hand.

Driving/String: This is a short glove with a leather palm, the back is knitted or made from another fabric, often knotted string. There is a buckle or stud fastener at the wrist.

White Kid Glove: A smart glove made in kid leather for formal day wear.

Cuff Guards: Decorative and protective guards for the wrists.

Hats
Page 154

Mahioli Helmet: A Hawaiian helmet from the eighteenth century, reminiscent of Greek helmets and beautifully curved in shape.

Kokoshnik Hat: A woman's hat from Russia, decorated with pearls and embroidery.

Chaperon with Dagges: See **chaperon**. This hat is much shorter, but is still draped and is decorated with the deep scalloped edge called dagges.

Bonnet: A medieval man's hat with a soft crown and firm brim.

Bashlik: This is of Russian origin and is worn like the liripipe, wrapped around the head like a turban.

Hood with Liripipe: The liripipe is the long trailing tail at the back of hoods from the thirteenth to the fifteenth centuries. It was also known as the 'tippet' which could be seen on women's headwear.

Chaperon: This is the name given to the hood that developed from the liripipe with its soft draping.

Phrygian Cap: A tall conical cap with a turn-up, worn by men from the Byzantine period, 530 BC.

Stocking Cap: Traditionally worn by sailors and fishermen, this hat became universally worn by workmen of all types up to the mid-nineteenth century. It was knitted and usually ended in a tassel.

Medieval Hunting Hat: The crown of this hat is asymmetrically shaped with a folded and long tapered brim hanging over the face (reminiscent of Robin Hood).

Negligée Cap: A full, drawn-up hat worn for sleeping.

Kokoshnik: A Russian hat, worn by women with a sarafan and loose shirt. See **kokoshnik hat**, an alternative decorated version.

Bicorn: A two-cornered hat that took over from the three-cornered hat, the tricorn. Used as part of ceremonial dress in the British, American and French navies.

Tricorn: A three-cornered hat. See the **bicorn**.

Papache: A Russian hat made from undyed sheepskin, usually found in black, white, brown or grey.

Halo Bonnet: This medieval hat had the brim turned back and decorated, so appearing to frame the face. It was often decorated with a plume and jewels.

Conical Cap: Similar to the **Phrygian cap**, but from Assyria around 850 BC.

Cap with Kissing Strings: A woman's cap with ties that are referred to as 'kissing strings' which tie under the chin.

Storm Hat: A warm, fur hat worn by men, similar to the **bolivar**.

Trembling Cap: A conical cap with a long tail.

Bolivar: A man's fur hat with a conical crown slightly cut off. It is named from Simon Bolivar, the early nineteenth century South American patriot.

Lama's Cap: From Manchuria, this decorative hat has ear flaps and silk ribbons. It is made in a variety of fabrics, the crown of brocade and the brim of cotton.

Alpine: A knitted cap for men worn for warmth in Austria.

Korean Hat and Band: A man's hat from Korea made from finely woven horsehair. The head band is worn under the hat.

Russian Hat: A conical hat with wide fur-trimmed brim worn by Russian men around 1850.

Coif: A linen cap from the early Middle Ages. Tied under the chin with strings. Worn by men and women as a night-cap or under another hat or cap.

Kala: A cap from Persia (now Iran) around the end of the nineteenth century. It is made from sheepskin and lined with calico.

Coolie: A conical shaped hat worn in China and made of straw.

Davy Crockett: A fur trapper's hat trimmed with racoon tails and named after Davy Crockett, the American trapper and explorer.

Tam-o'-shanter: This hat is rather like the beret but fuller. It is made of brushed wool plaid and named from the hero of the poem by Robert Burns.

Scottish: A traditional cap worn with the kilt.

Tyrolean/Eiger: This is a soft felt hat, usually dark green (loden) banded with a ribbon and decorated with a feather.

Page 155

Trooper: This fleece-lined hat has a peak and ear flaps which can be folded back until needed in bad weather.

G.I. Helmet Liner: This is a knitted helmet liner worn for comfort by the American armed forces. 'G.I' is an abbreviation of Government Issue and has become a slang term for anything relating to the American army.

Cloth Cap: This cap is made from checked wool and worn traditionally by British working men, epitomised by the cartoon character, Andy Capp.

Beatle Cap: A cap that was worn and made famous by the Beatles in the 1960s.

Motoring Cap: This is an early twentieth century cap worn while motoring, usually because the first cars were not covered. This example is made from leather.

Fez: Originating from Turkey, the fez is a brimless, truncated cone shaped cap with a tassel for decoration.

Pith Helmet/Safari: This hat was worn by the British army in India. It is made of pith cork from the sponge wood tree covered in white cotton and lined in green. The cork acts as insulation against the sun and is relatively impervious to water.

Field: A fabric hat with a leather peak worn by American armed forces in the 'field'.

Bobble Hat with Pom-Pom: This is a knitted cap with a ribbed cuff. It is usually striped and topped off for decoration with a wool pom-pom, that is, a ball of tufted wool.

Beret: This is a circular piece of cloth, usually felt, that is drawn together into a narrow band. The little spike on the top is called the 'tontarra'.

Plantation: This hat is traditionally worn in the cotton plantations and is made of cotton.

Nehru/Service: A fabric hat that folds flat when not in use.

It was worn by the American armed forces and also by Pandit Nehru, the Indian Swarajist leader who became the first prime minister of the Republic of India. Nehru gave inspiration to many garments – the suit, the collar, the jacket.

Muffin: This is a man's round, fabric hat with a flat crown and narrow upright brim worn with ribbons at the back.

French Sailor Cap: This is a peaked cap made in fabric and worn by French sailors.

Top Hat: A tall crowned hat with a flat top and narrow brim worn for formal occasions.

Ten Gallon with Hat Band: This is the archetypal American cowboy hat made from felt.

Bush Hat: This is a fabric hat with top-stitching on the brim and eyelets to circulate air.

Smoking Cap: This eastern influenced cap would be worn by the Edwardian gentleman along with a velvet smoking jacket.

Breton: This hat was originally worn by the peasants of Brittany. It is a felt or straw hat with the brim turned back evenly all round.

Stovepipe: This is an exaggerated version of the top hat. It has a straight crown and smaller brim, popular in the nineteenth century.

Australian Military with Puggaree Hat Band: As the name suggests, this felt hat is worn by the Australian military. The puggaree is a band wrapped around the crown of the hat, although it is also the term for the Hindu turban, made from yards of fabric wrapped around the head in a variety of styles (see also **pagri**).

Stetson: The same as the **ten gallon hat**, but a better quality version produced by John B. Stetson, a hatmaker from Philadelphia in the 1870s.

School Cap: This is a rounded peaked cap worn by school boys. The hat is panelled and frequently the panels are alternate in colour to match school colours.

Bowler/Derby (US): This is a hard, dome-shaped, felt hat appearing in 1850 and designed by William Bowler. The hat is known as the derby by Americans because it was worn by the Earl of Derby at Epsom Downs.

Baseball Cap: A cap that was named after the American game of baseball and worn universally. The cap is made of mesh fabric at the back, with an adjustable strapping for a good fit. The fabric front and fabric covered peak are often decorated with badges and team logos.

Helmet with Chin Strap: A stiff hat made from a variety of fabrics and shapes, here with a chin strap. The helmet can also be rigid as motorcycle helmets etc.

Sombrero and Barbiqueio (Chin Strap): This is the South American version of the cowboy hat. The barbiqueio is the chin strap used to keep the sombrero on the head whilst riding.

Fedora: This is a soft felt hat, with a centre crease from back to front on the crown. It is related to the Tyrolean hat.

Homburg: Manufactured in Homburg in soft felt. The hat has a tapered crown with a stiff brim and ribbon band.

Deerstalker: Used for sports and travelling, this hat is made from checked wool with ear flaps. Closely associated with the character Sherlock Holmes.

Balaclava: Named after the sea port of Balaclava, this heavy knitted helmet was first adopted by the British army for warmth in the Crimean War. It was also made for soldiers in World Wars I and II.

Sou'wester: An oilskin hat worn by fishermen. It has a sloping back to cover the neck and protect against stormy weather. Traditionally it is yellow in colour for visibility during storms.

Bushman: A felt hat that is worn in the Australian bush.

Pork Pie: A small hat with a narrow brim and shallow crown with band.

Domed Cricket: A straw hat originally worn during cricket matches.

Panama: Made of hand plaited straw, the hat was named after Panama where it was marketed but never actually made.

Trilby: A soft felt hat with a brushed surface similar to the Tyrolean hat.

Ski Mask: A fine knitted hood similar to the balaclava, but also covering the face with holes for the mouth and eyes. Used to protect the face when skiing.

Page 156

Gibson Girl: A hat that was worn by women in the paintings by American artist, Charles Dana Gibson. It is similar to the picture hat.

Lampshade Straw: A straw hat shaped like a lampshade with a very shallow crown and fabric ties.

Gypsy Straw: A small straw hat worn by women and decorated with flowers which was popular in the nineteenth century.

Bergère/Milkmaid: This is a large straw hat with a low crown and average width brim.

Cartwheel: A wide-brimmed hat, the brim being the same width all the way round, with a low, flat crown. It is made from straw.

Boater: Originally worn on the river for punting etc. It is made from straw with a flat crown and shallow brim.

Picture: This is a wide-brimmed hat richly trimmed and similar to the **Gibson Girl**.

Gainsborough: Called a Gainsborough, because this style of hat was regularly painted by Thomas Gainsborough in the late eighteenth century. It was made from black velvet or taffeta with ostrich plumes and ribbons.

Gob's/Sailor: A white cotton twill cap worn in the American Navy. This is a more modern version of the sailor/pie plate/hat.

Sailor/Pie Plate: Worn by sailors in the American Navy in the nineteenth century. This hat has a very flat top and was made from blue wool for winter wear and white cotton for summer.

Capeline/Skimmer: A wide, soft-brimmed, leghorn hat faced with silk (leghorn being a particularly fine straw). It was worn over a lawn cap and tied with ribbons. It was of English origin and popular around the middle of the eighteenth century.

Beehive Bonnet: Reminiscent of a beehive shape, this straw hat has floral decoration and is tied under the chin with ribbons. It dates from the early 1800s.

Slouch: This hat is made from felt with a rolling brim and two ribbons hanging at the back. It is of Hungarian origin.

Riding Bowler: As the **bowler** hat but worn by women with a veil. Used for riding in the late nineteenth century.

Bucket: Made from felt or straw this hat resembles an inverted bucket.

Sun Hat: Bright and colourful, contemporary, printed sun hat for protection against the sun.

Sugar Loaf: The sugar loaf has a high conical crown with a broad brim. It was derived from a copotain, which had a narrower brim.

Half Hat: This hat covers only part of the head. It is usually worn at the back of the head and decorated with feathers and flowers over a silk or fur base. It is pinned in place with a hat pin.

Riding Hat: A hard, domed shaped hat worn for protection when horse riding.

Cloche: A small, well-fitting hat, covering the neck and the forehead. Very popular in the 1920s when hair was bobbed. Made in felt with a grosgrain band.

Pill Box: This small and simple hat is worn on the back of the head and made of fabric, the hat has a flat crown and no brim.

Wimple: A piece of fabric worn on the head and allowed to hang to the shoulders, usually fixed with a crown or other head band.

Skull Cap/Juliet Cap: A small circular cap or calotte worn on the back of the head and which can be richly decorated.

Watteau with Hat Pin: A straw or felt hat which can be decorated with ostrich plumes and ribbons. It is featured in the paintings of Jean Antoine Watteau. The hat has no brim or crown and is more like a stiffened disc of fabric. The hat pin is used to pin hats to the hair to prevent them from blowing away, or to style and wear the hat in a particular way. Hat pins themselves can be very decorative.

Eugenie: A small pill-box type hat worn with plumes. Named after the Empress Eugenie who was married to Napoleon III and the centre of a luxurious court in mid-nineteenth century France.

Hair Bag: A decorated bag, made in taffeta and decorated with gold braids, for covering the hair of a Tartar woman.

Pagri: An Indian turban, made from a length of cloth wrapped around the head (see also **puggaree**).

Kaffiyeh with Egal: A traditional Arab head dress made from linen, cotton, wool or silk. It could be plain or patterned is still worn today, often with western clothing. The egal holds the kaffiyeh on the head. It can be highly decorated and consists of two or three cords made into a band.

Taboosh with Tassel: An Egyptian hat for men, similar to the fez but with a more waisted shape.

Headrail/Couvrechief: An Anglo-Saxon head covering, being a piece of fabric draped over the head and held in place with a band. 'Couvrechief' was the Norman term for the same headdress.

Litham: A veil or scarf worn by Arab women in public to cover their faces. It is also worn in a similar way by men in desert tribes, such as the Tuaregs, as protection from sand storms.

Khat: An Egyptian headdress from around 1350 BC, made from striped linen and best known as the headdress worn by Tutankhamen.

Page 157

Caul: A netted silk or wool cap for women, covered with a trellis of decorative cord and popular in the medieval period.

Crispinette: A mesh, snood-like article worn with a jewelled crown.

Mob Cap: This eighteenth-century cap fitted loosely on the head without fastenings. It was made of cambric and muslin with a puffed caul (a net covering for the head) and frilled border. Modern variants can be elasticated for a good fit.

Widow's Peak: A triangle of black fabric set just above the forehead to indicate mourning. This was worn in the eighteenth and nineteenth centuries.

Chignon Bonnet: A fabric hat with ribbons encasing the hair and strapped under the chin, it was worn around 1800.

Snood with Straw: This is a fabric bag to hold the hair loosely. It is often quite decorative and is worn here with a straw hat.

Fontange: A tall, stiff headdress of the seventeenth century made from starched lawn and wire with lace and ribbon trims.

Mantilla and Comb: A lace shawl draped over the head and held in place with a high comb, popular in Spain from the seventeenth century and still worn as part of traditional Spanish costume.

Bonnet à la Syrienne: Developed from a Syrian bonnet called 'the tantur' over which was spread a veil. This tall medieval hat was worn throughout Europe.

Attifet Headdress: A close-fitting heart-shaped headdress, trimmed with lace and worn in the sixteenth and seventeenth centuries. The front edges of the headdress are wired to hold the shape.

Fitted Hood: As the name suggests, a hood that fits the shape of the head being constructed with seams or made in a stretch fabric.

Hood: Usually made from woven or knitted fabric, the hood is a covering for the head and is attached to a garment at the neck.

Alice Band: A stretch fabric band, worn around the head to style hair. Made popular by the illustrations by Tenniel from Lewis Carroll's *Alice in Wonderland*.

Turban: A length of fabric wrapped around the head, originating as menswear from India and the Near East, and adopted, in richly decorated form, as a hat style by western women.

Calash: This is a hooped bonnet that folded when not worn. Made in fabric and tied under the chin, the bonnet was named after a French folding carriage called the caleche.

Horned Headdress: A headdress from the Netherlands popular in the fifteenth century. Usually worn with the veil draped over the top of the horns.

Linen Hood with Lappets: This is a cloth hat (linen), with lappets, which are tails of fabric hanging from the hat and wrapped and tied over the top of the head. Popular around the 1520s.

Sports Head Band: A sweat band for the head when partaking in sporting activities, it can also keep the hair out of the wearer's eyes.

Bonnet: A brimless hat wrapped around the head, often made of fabric, which ties under the chin.

Crown Hat with Barbette: The barbette was a piece of cloth wrapped around a woman's head from the top of the head to under the chin. It was held in place with a crown hat and was worn in the mid thirteenth century.

Steeple Hennin: A tall hat that often reached exaggerated proportions and was worn, occasionally, with a veil. See also **bonnet à la Syrienne**.

Mortar Board: This is a stiffened cap with a square board on top worn at academic ceremonies with the **hood cape** and **academic gown**.

Reflective Head Band: A reflective head band worn for safety when cycling in the dark. It will fit over the cycling helmet.

Hood Cape: This hood is part of academic dress at award ceremonies for graduates. It is worn over the **academic gown** and may be a variety of colours and designs depending on the designation of the degree and the university to which it belongs. The liripipe is of medieval origin but all that is left here is a stump, a shortened version.

See **hood with liripipe**.

Cycling Helmet: A hard hat made from compressed polystyrene with a moulded plastic cover. This hat is intended to protect the wearer from head injury in cycling accidents. It is fastened by webbing straps that wrap under the chin.

Face Mask: Worn mainly by women from the sixteenth century, it was meant to protect the face when riding or in poor weather. It was very fashionable in the eighteenth and nineteenth centuries as party wear to conceal the identity of the wearer.

Face Mask with Ventilation Holes: A recent development, the mask is worn over the face by cyclists who ride through polluted cities on their way to and from work.

Little Hennin: A steeple shaped headdress, the little hennin is shorter than the steeple hennin and does not finish in a point.

Head Scarf/Babushka/Shale: A square of fabric folded and wrapped around the head to fasten, with narrow corners, in a knot under the chin. When fastened at the nape of the neck it is known as a 'platok'.

Toque: This is a soft, brimless hat, made of fabric.

Belts
Page 158

Obi: The Japanese sash wrapped around the body and tied at the back in a large flat bow or butterfly bow (inside the bow is the small cushion for padding called the obiage).

Baldric: A wide silk sash or leather belt worn over the right shoulder and fastened on the left hip to carry a sword or bugle.

Sporran and Belt: From the Scottish Highlands, this pouch is worn over the kilt. It is made of leather, or it may also be made from fur.

Knotted Girdle: See **girdle**. This example has a series of knots and ends in a crucifix, probably belonging to a nun.

Sash/Cestus: In classical dress a cestus is a sash, a long piece of fabric wrapped and tied around the body.

Girdle: A belt for the waist or hips dating from the early Middle Ages. A woman's girdle would hang down her centre front and end in a book, pomander, mirror or jewel.

Cordelière: A French expression for a girdle made from rope and worn mostly by monks, ending in a knot and tassels.

Chain Belt: A loose belt made from numerous chain links and hooked together to fasten.

Schoolboy Belt: An elasticated belt, with a stripe running through it, fastened with a metal 'S' shaped interlocking clip. Worn, as the name suggests, by schoolboys.

Cummerbund: A wide sash of fabric, often pleated and wrapped around the body. Worn instead of a waistcoat for formal wear.

Cinch: This wide belt is made from strong elastic and achieves the effect of cinching the waist.

Belt Box: Bags and purses have been attached to belts frequently throughout the ages. This example shows a Bronze Age belt box found in Denmark. The box is large enough to hold small valuables or sewing equipment.

Bias Tie: A fabric belt cut on the bias or the cross, then wrapped around the body achieving a hugging fit.

Waistcoat Belt: A cross between the cummerbund and the waistcoat, it is belted at the back and has pockets like the waistcoat.

Cartridge Belt: A hunter's belt, with room to carry numerous gun cartridges.

Wide Belt: An extra wide belt for cinching in the waist. It can be made from leather or a woven fabric.

Ruched Belt: A rectangular piece of fabric is drawn through a buckle to fasten it creating a ruched effect.

Contour: A shaped belt that can be worn on the hips.

Martingale/Half Belt: This belt is usually fixed into the side seams of a garment and lies on the back of the garment.

Webbing: A strong, narrow belt worn by the armed forces with a clip-type buckle.

Bustle Effect Scarf: Here a large scarf is tied to effect a bustle.

Jewelled Metal Girdle: An English example from about 1360, this metal belt is worn slung low on the hips over a doublet or tunic. It is heavily jewelled.

Self-fasten (D-rings): D-rings work in pairs and the belt is drawn through one ring and then is pulled backwards through the other.

Straight Belt: A straight piece of leather or fabric is pulled to the required size and buckled.

Rouleau Tie: A 'string' effect belt, with a single tie.

Spaghetti Belt: Three or more string ties form the spaghetti belt.

Purse: A leather belt with box-like leather purses hanging from it.

Châtelaine with Étui: Châtelaine is a French word to describe 'the mistress of the castle'. She wore her keys hanging from her waist and eventually her name was applied to the waist hung belt. Étui is also a French word which describes a small case or box containing small toilet and sewing articles which is hung from the châtelaine. Popular from the seventeenth century.

Scarf Belt: A large rectangle of fabric draped around the hips and tied into a knot, similar to the bustle effect scarf.

Stable Belt: A belt used by the armed forces and having stripes woven through it. The fastening is made from two leather straps and buckles, with a leather reinforcement.

Firearm: A leather belt meant to carry a small gun and ammunition.

Sam Browne: Designed by the British General, Sir Samuel Browne, a wide leather belt is supported by a narrow strap passing over the right shoulder. It was worn by army officers in World War I.

Neckwear
Page 159

Fichu: This is a length of fabric worn around the neck and shoulders and used as a fill-in on low-cut gowns.

Spotted Handkerchief: A square handkerchief covered in polka dots, usually red and white, but can be any colour.

Ascot: A cravat with wide, square ends, folded and kept in place with a tie pin.

Kipper Tie: An exaggerated tie popular in the late 1960s.

String Tie: A simple string effect tie which is tied in a bow at the front.

Lariat Tie with Aiglet Points: A string tie, fixed by a sliding ornament. The points are finished by small metal cones called aiglets.

Tie: The tie is worn with the shirt, and a variety of knots may be used to tie it. Fashion is reflected in the width, length, colour and pattern of the tie.

Flat Scarf: A flat piece of fabric is attached to a band to hold it round the neck.

Cravat with Pin: A rectangle of fabric is wrapped around the neck and fixed with a pin.

De Joinville: A broad, wide-spreading bow with square fringed edges.

Steinkirk: A loosely tied scarf with the ends drawn through a buttonhole or tucked into a shirt.

Chemisette: This garment is made from muslin and used as a fill-in for a low-cut gown.

Dickie: A starched shirt-front with collar attached which can be worn for formal wear.

Napoleon Tie/Corsican: A narrow, violet coloured necktie, wrapped around the neck and crossed over at the front, the ends are then fastened under the arms and tied at the back or fixed to braces.

Four-in-hand: A long necktie with wide ends that ties in a knot with the ends hanging vertically. It is named after the horse drivers who could manage a 'four-in-hand'.

Croatian: A simple, long piece of fabric tied in a knot and left to hang, not as rigid as a four in hand.

1950s Tie: These ties were designed to conceal surprise images in the lining, the front of the tie would be patterned and colourful.

Muffler: A woollen scarf worn around the neck for warmth.

Bow Tie: Used in formal wear, the bow can be fixed and tied around the neck or can be tied each time it is worn. Achieving an even bow can be something of a skill.

Cloud: A filmy scarf of wool or silk.

Neckerchief: A square of fabric folded and tied around the neck. Usually made in bright colours or patterns.

Face Muffler: A handkerchief sized square, folded diagonally, placed over the mouth and tied at the back of the neck. Worn during stormy or dusty weather for protection.

Schoolboy Scarf: A long and narrow, knitted and striped scarf worn by school children, often as part of a regulation uniform.

Stock: A high neckcloth of linen stiffened with pasteboard which was tied or buckled at the back of the neck.

Yankee Necktie: A form of stock with pleats either side of the centre front, the narrow ends are brought forward and tied in a 'Gordian knot'.

Military Stock: This stock is stiffened by leather and tied or buckled at the back. The stock is usually white in colour for civilians and black for the military.

Incroyable Cravat: A cravat inspired by the Directoire period, this being when a committee of five men governed France from 1795 to 1799 ending the 'Reign of Terror'. Napoleon ended the Directoire and made himself First Consul. See also Outerwear – **incroyable coat**.

Feather Boa: A long scarf covered with soft feathers (or which can also be made of fur, tulle or lace) usually worn with evening dress. It is wrapped around the neck and allowed to hang down to the knees. The name 'boa' is derived from the boa constrictor snake.

Boots
Page 160

Guard: This style of boot was worn by both Wellington and Napoleon and officers of the European armies in the early nineteenth century. It is made of leather with a square cut top and is chamois lined. It has loops to pull it on and spurs for horse riding.

Slashed: Worn in the late sixteenth century, for a full description of the fashion see **slashed trunk hose**.

Spatterdash: Medieval, high, leather leggings with multi-button fastening. See also **spats**.

Bucket: This is a thigh high boot doubled over to form a deep cuff.

Cavalier: A wide-legged boot with falling tops, named after the cavaliers who were loyal to Charles I in the English Civil War.

Gaiter/Spat: Spat is short for spatterdash. They are worn with Oxfords or pumps and made of broadcloth in white, grey or tan. They are buttoned at the sides.

Derby Boot: A lace-up ankle length boot, the toe and the quarters are overlaid and stitched on to the vamp. The vamp covers the middle of the foot, the quarters the back of the shoe up to the vamp.

Jack (English): Popular in the seventeenth and eighteenth centuries, this boot was large enough to wear a slipper or shoe inside it. It was made of jack leather – a waxed leather coated with tar.

Woman's Walking: This example is an early twentieth-century woman's walking boot with a multi-eyelet lace-up front for a good, leg-hugging fit.

Ladies' Side Button: An early twentieth-century, side-button ladies' boot, reminiscent of the gaiter or spat.

Postilion with Gambado: An eighteenth-century black, leather boot, with a seventeenth-century gambado moulded to fit over the boot and attached to the stirrup.

Desert: A short, suede ankle boot, usually light tan in colour.

Shenandoah: A type of cowboy boot.

Ankle with Stiletto: A woman's ankle boot with a stiletto heel and elasticated gusset to help pull the boot on.

Pirate: A strappy leather boot in the 'pirate' style. Popular in the late 1970s and early 1980s particularly the youth market in street wear.

Chelsea: Generally a boot with an elasticated inset, here shown as a lace up.

Mukluk/Slipper Sock: The term is of Arctic origin. This example is a knitted sock with a sole, but it can also be an Arctic boot lined with fur and made of sealskin. See **arctic mukluk**.

Wet Look Platform: This example is made from 'wet look' leather (not really a leather but a stretch PVC fabric). It dates from the mid 1970s and has a zip fastener up the inside leg. See also **platform with sling-back**.

Courrèges: This boot was designed by Courrèges in the 1960s. There is a peep hole in the toe and a decorative ribbon around the top of the boot.

Yves Saint Laurent: Yves Saint Laurent took inspiration from the paintings of Mondrian for these boots in white, red, blue and yellow.

Tabi-toe Boot: Designed by Martin Margiela, this boot is based on the traditional Japanese sock with divided toe which is meant to be worn with thong sandals.

Platform: This leather zip-up boot was very popular in the early 1970s with its trade mark upper worn with maxi, midi and mini skirts.

Thigh High: A long-legged boot reaching mid-thigh.

Page 161

Fisherman's Wader: A long, waterproof boot, usually rubber, which has straps to fit it to a waterproof garment.

Wellington: A waterproof boot worn originally by the Duke of Wellington, here the boot is fleece lined for warmth. See also CHILDRENSWEAR – **Wellington**.

Paratrooper/Jump: A substantial leather boot used for parachute jumping.

Camouflage Hunting: Used by the armed forces, this boot has a khaki camouflage pattern. It has a fabric leg and leather upper.

Work Boot: A heavy duty leather boot with a steel toe for protection.

Safety Bike: A standard boot for riding motorcycles. Extra protection is afforded by the steel toecap.

Jodhpur: This boot is worn when horse riding, with jodhpur trousers. It is fastened with a wrap-around strap and buckle.

Riding Boot: An ankle length boot with elasticated inset, worn in horse riding. There are also longer versions.

Field Boot: A leather boot from the 1940s, it combines buckles and straps with lace-ups further down the boot.

Doctor Marten – Airwair™: A leather boot with twelve eyelet holes, the soles are air cushioned and were developed by Dr Marten. The boot has cult status and is universally worn. It is now also available in a variety of fabrics and print finishes.

Cowboy: Worn by American cowboys, this boot has square toes and is often decoratively top stitched.

Spurs: These spurs are worn by American cowboys and are used to urge the horse they are riding onwards. They are strapped to the cowboy boot.

Cowboy/Cancan: Designed by Alexander McQueen, this boot reveals the heel and is laced up, down the back, taking its inspiration from the cancan girl and traditional cowboy boot.

Maine Hunting™: This is a trade name for an American boot that is waterproof and worn for walking and hunting.

Hiking/Mountain: A hard wearing, comfortable, waterproof boot used for hiking.

Timberland™: This is a trade name for a leather, lace-up boot used for general wear and walking. It has a padded ankle and is usually tan in colour.

Dirt Bike (Steel Toe): A customised motorcycle boot with a steel toe for extra protection. The customising consists of the stitched logos, the dark straps and toe.

Chinese: This Chinese boot is made in three colours of brocade with a kid foot.

Cossack: A leather Cossack boot from the 1850s, this boot has a shaped toe.

Legging Hose: From Siberia, this boot is part of ceremonial dress. It is made from reindeer skin and decorated with leather mosaics.

Lapland: This boot is from Lapland and has indented decoration on the front in the natural coloured leather.

Ug Boot: Derived from the caveman look, the boot is quite chunky and the upper is completely executed in fake fur.

Leather Sock: From East Siberia this sock-like boot is made from soft leather and is fur lined. It fastens to the wearer's belt.

Chinese with Felt Sole: A Chinese boot, the upper is made of leather and the sole of felt.

Arctic Mukluk: This is a canvas boot with a leather sole from the 1940s. It has a crossover, lace-up effect fastening and is worn over another leather boot.

Kurdish Leather: This short but wide boot is decorated with a tassel and is Kurdish in origin.

Korean: A wide-topped leather boot with fur trim from Korea, it has a distinctive curled up toe.

Shoes
Page 162

High-Tongue: A medieval shoe known for its high tongue at the front. It is a flat shoe with no heel.

Poulaine: A long pointed-toe shoe from the late fourteenth century.

Persian Slipper: A curved sole shoe from Persia, decorated with embroidery on suede.

Piked: A medieval shoe with long, pointed toes. Sometimes the toe became so long that it had to be supported by a gold chain attached to the ankles or knees.

Rose Window: A medieval shoe with cut-outs allowing multi-coloured underlays to show through.

Cresida Sandal: An ancient Roman sandal, made from leather wrapped around the foot and ankle, with cut-outs for lacing and a cut-away toe.

Moroccan Slipper: A slipper from Morocco made in leather with gold thread embroidery.

Babouche Slipper: A Turkish slipper made in fabric or leather and decorated with spangles, beads and metal threads. Nowadays the term refers to a soft leather slipper where the toes are squared off.

Caliga Sandal: An ancient Roman sandal made from leather thongs tied across the foot and up the ankle.

Chopine: Designed for keeping feet out of the sand and mud, chopines are made of wood and originate in Turkey.

Knob Style: A man's sandal, flat soled with a platform at the toe and heel. It is held to the foot by the knob on the top which is gripped between the toes.

Pampootie: A fur and skin moccasin style shoe from the Isles of Aran, from the nineteenth century. It has a lace trim which fastens over the foot.

Hobnailed: A woman's shoe from Korea, very blunt in shape and trimmed with fabric.

Kub-Kob: A Turkish shoe made with inlaid mother of pearl and silver on a rigid sole.

Chinese Shoe (Bound Feet): A short, decorative shoe worn by high-born Chinese women whose feet had been bound from girlhood to keep them small.

Pantofle/Medieval Overshoe: A medieval overshoe worn to protect the normal shoe.

Moccasin: A soft leather shoe without a heel worn by North American Indians. The sides and sole are made in one piece.

Clog: Development from the patten, the clog is made from leather nailed to a shaped wooden sole.

Patten: A wooden soled shoe, on a raised metal stand, with leather straps, worn on top of normal footwear to protect it from foul weather.

Sabot: This is a shoe shaped from a solid piece of wood. It originated in France but is now more closely associated with Holland.

Palm Leaf Sandal: An ancient Egyptian sandal made from woven palm leaves. The foot slides through a woven palm strap and is protected by a tongue that wraps over the top of the foot from the toe.

Baxea Sandal: An ancient woven, flat sandal with straps and heel for a good fit.

Black Jack: This is a seventeenth century English shoe, with a high, square heel and toe with an exaggerated tongue. See also **jack boot**.

Galosh (Men's): This is an overshoe made from rubber and lined with canvas. Like the patten it is designed to protect normal shoes from poor weather conditions.

Shetland Clog: From the late nineteenth century, this clog comes from the Shetland Islands. The clog is shaped to the foot and a leather upper is nailed to the wooden sole. A piece of leather or metal strip is attached to the sole with brass nails that do not rust to protect the clog from damp.

Men's Sandal: This sandal has cut-out uppers and a 'T' bar fastener with buckle.

Spat: Short for spatterdashes and worn with **Oxfords**, spats are made from broadcloth in white, grey or tan and button at the sides. They have elastic to wrap under the foot. See the longer version under Boots.

Galosh (Women's): This is a plastic galosh that covers the entire shoe. See **Galosh (Men's)** for a fuller description.

Blucher (US): the American name for a lace up shoe. On this example there are 'wing tips' on the toe.

Jesus Sandal: This sandal consists of a sole held on the foot by two sets of straps. One of these wraps around the ankle and the other across the base of the toes.

Saddle: In this shoe a piece of leather is laid over the vamp and includes the lacing.

Co-respondent: These shoes are manufactured in two tone white buck and brown calf and other contrasts. Usually a low- or mid-heeled shoe. It was popular in the 1920s and 1930s.

Slip-on: There is no fastening on this shoe, it is simply slipped on.

Dress: A plain shoe worn with formal dress.

Oxford: This shoe has been associated with the under-graduates of Oxford. The vamp, covering the front of the foot, is stitched on top of the quarters – the back of the shoe up to the vamp.

Balmoral: 'Bal' is an abbreviation of Balmoral. It is a low-heeled shoe with a lace-up fastening almost reaching the toe.

Loafer with Tassels: This is a slip-on shoe with a low heel and tassels on the front. It originates in Norway.

Brogue: A pattern of stitching and punching is the hallmark of this heavy classic style shoe.

Page 163

Winkle Picker: A shoe with a sharply pointed toe – named after the sharp pick used to eat winkles.

Brothel Creeper/Beetle Crusher: A thick crepe soled shoe worn in the 1950s by Teddy Boys. The upper is made of suede or leather.

Rockports™: A contemporary shoe popular with youth, chunky soles, padded and reflective detail highlight the heel and vamp.

Dance: This is a shoe cut in one piece, with a lace-up front. It has a flat heel and sole and is used for dancing.

Gymnastic: This is a specialist sports shoe worn in the gymnasium. It has an elasticated inset for a comfortable fit.

Platform with Sling-back: A deep-soled shoe of a fashion from the early 1970s that sometimes reached ridiculous proportions. It is shown here with a sling-back that hooks around the back of the ankle and a wedge heel.

No Heel: These shoes have sculptured wedges with springs and steel soles allowing the removal of the heel. This was part of an experiment carried out in the 1960s.

Peep-toe Wedge with Sling-back: With this shoe the toe is cut away and the wedge is a continuation of the heel. See **platform with sling-back** for information on the sling-back.

Ankle Strap: A shoe, any style, with a strap that wraps fully around the ankle and fastens with a small buckle. This example has a small platform and wedge heel, that is, the platform and heel are joined together.

Louis Heel: The sole of the shoe is cut to continue under the instep of the shoe and attach to the front (breast) of the heel in one continuous shape. This heel can be of any height, or shape. The term 'Louis' is, however, generally applied to a high heel with a curved waist which flares at the base.

Huarache: A shoe made from interwoven leather thonging. The example here has a sling-back and low heel.

Espadrille: A woven or plaited, straw shoe.

Stiletto Heel: These are long, pointed heels on women's court shoes, worn for special and formal occasions, sometimes as day wear. They have the effect of lengthening the leg and so are considered very attractive. On the other hand, prolonged wear can cause medical problems because the body weight is thrown forward and the heels themselves can damage wooden flooring because the weight is concentrated in a small area (see **Canadian Snowshoe** for contrast).

d'Orsay: An open-waisted shoe, that is the toe and heel taper away towards the centre of the shoe.

Court: This is any kind of woman's shoe that can be stepped into without straps or lacing.

Mule: These are feminine slippers for use in the house (mules are also worn outside in the summer). They have a decorative toe and are backless. They may have any height of heel.

Ballet Pump: This shoe is used in ballet dancing as the name suggest. Usually it is made in kid leather. The bow at the front is in fact part of a drawstring allowing a snug fit.

Stacked Heel: The heel is formed by layering, bonding and shaping materials such as leather or wood.

T-Bar: The strapping of this shoe is shaped like a 'T' from the front. The sling-back is threaded through a strap coming from the toe up the centre front and fastened with a buckle.

Cuban Heel: This is derived from the heel worn by South American gauchos (cowboys). These were short and straight and enabled the gaucho to wear stirrups.

Ghillie: The cut-outs on the front of this shoe form the loops through which the shoe is laced. Originally a Scottish dancing shoe, it was popularised by Edward VIII and may also be known as the 'Prince of Wales' shoe.

Cloven Toe: Jeremy Scott designed this shoe with the cloven toe. It evokes satanic imagery and at first glance of the profile looks quite normal.

Opera Pump: A low-cut, high-heeled shoe, cut from one piece of fabric or leather.

Invisible Shoe: These shoes were made in Perspex and the original 'invisible shoe' of 1947 was designed and patented by Salvatore Ferragamo.

Brass Shoe: Designed by Ferragamo and dating from 1930, he pushed designing the shoe and heel to its limits with use of materials such as brass.

Simple Sandal: This very simple design is by Sergio Rossi and has a supple leather footbed (following the shape of the foot) with very fine straps. The heel is made of wood and metal.

V-throat: The front of this shoe is shaped like a 'V'.

Spectator: A court shoe constructed with two contrasting colours.

Mary Jane: A low-heeled shoe with a rounded toe, cut all in one piece but with a bar strap and buckle to fasten.

Flip Flop: A simple, rubber-soled sandal, with strapping that fits between the big and second toes.

Canadian Snowshoe: The snowshoe is an oval framework of bent wood, strung in a net pattern with strips of waterproof thonging. When the wearers' boots are strapped to such shoes they can walk in soft snow without sinking as their weight is spread over a larger area (see **stiletto** for contrast).

Japanese Snowshoe: See **Canadian Snowshoe** for a full description. This snowshoe is made of bent wood and strappings and was made in the early 1900s. It is about 21 inches (53 cm) long.

Sports Shoe
Page 164

These shoes are grouped together because they are for use in sports or they have used a sporting influence in their design.

Hi-top Trainer: A development of the training shoe by thickening the sole, enlarging the tongue and raising the sides to ankle height. Decoration is added in the form of a detachable medallion and extra stripings.

American Football: A sports shoe for playing American football. It has decorative stripings that are know as 'go faster stripes'.

Football Lineman (US): A sports shoe as the name suggests. It has a studded sole and is slightly shaped.

Training: A popular sports shoe worn generally, often with decorative and bright stripings called 'go faster stripes'.

Aerobic: A specialist sports shoe along the same lines as the tennis, training and football shoes.

Retro Trainer: An early 1980s trainer, slimline and simple in design, now a design classic, recently enjoying a resurrection. Manufacturers labels, of note, were Puma and Adidas, later followed by Reebok and Nike.

Boat/Deck: A canvas sports shoe with a lace-up front and rubber sole, worn on boat decks originally.

Weight Lifting: As the name suggests, a leather sports shoe used in weight lifting. It has a reinforced heel and decorative stripings running across the top of the shoe.

Bicycling with Sole: A shoe with a very curved sole and no heel. It is fastened with lace-ups and a Velcro™ strap. The sole of the shoe is shown because there is a facility for clipping specialist pedals into the shoe whilst riding the bicycle. The shoe is removed from the pedal by a quick twist of the foot.

Cycling Shoe Cover: This cover is Velcro™ fastened over the cycling shoe to protect it from poor weather conditions.

Peep-toe Trainer: The toe piece has been removed from this shoe, but it still has the same function as the training shoe.

Distressed Trainer: The normal trainer detail updated by the use of a distressed painted canvas and reflective ribbons criss-crossing over the top of the shoe.

Roller Blade Effect: The conventional upper/vamp in suede is updated with a deep, rippling, rubber base, reminiscent of roller blades.

Baseball/Converse Allstars™: This is a trade name for a baseball boot that is made of canvas with a rubber sole. The baseball boot has been popular casual wear for many years but has been recently usurped by the popularity of the training shoe.

Boxing: A lower-calf-length boot with multi-eyelet fastening, it has been used as a fashion accessory as well as for the sport of boxing.

Side-fastening Trainer: The normal lace-up fastening is moved over to the side, to give a smooth surface over the top of the vamp – considered useful in contemporary football boots.

Neoprene™ Trainer: A sling-back sports shoe ideal for beachwear and paddling due to the waterproof neoprene.

Backless Allstars™: A development of the Converse Allstars boot by going to the extreme of removing the back heel, giving a mule effect.

Platform Trainer: Even the training shoe has not managed to avoid the 'platform'.

Strap-fastening Trainer™: A series of crossover straps with Velcro™ secure the shoe into place.

Trainer Mule: Suede upper with a contemporary sports shoe sole. The shoe has an elasticated inset for a snug fit and an open back.

Après Sport Sandal: A single strap sandal, fastened with Velcro™, meant for wearing after sports to allow the feet to relax. It has a textured sole.

Golf: A stout brogue shoe worn on the golf course, it has punched decoration and a tasselled flap over the front.

Soccer Boot: A shoe for playing European football. It has a firm sole with screw-in studs and is usually made from leather.

High Heeled Sneaker: Derived from sports shoes and designed by Jean Paul Gaultier, feminised by the high heel, this is a canvas boot with rubber toe.

Platform Trainers Exaggerated: An extreme derivation of the trainer – retaining little of the practical design of the sports shoe. Worn by such as 'The Spice Girls' in the late 1990s.

Hosiery
Page 165

Tights: They may be very finely knitted garments or very chunky garments or anything in between. Tights are a continuation of the brief and the stocking.

Garter: These are used for keeping up socks and stockings. The garter can be decorative as well as functional and was originally a tie before the invention of elastic. See **fringed sash garter**.

Sock and Suspender: Men's knitted socks held up by suspenders which sit below the knee.

Over Knee Socks: These are knitted stockings which finish above the knee, but are not as long as conventional stockings.

Seamed Stockings: A seam of construction runs up the back of the stocking and, being no longer a necessary fashion feature, this is seen as a desirable fashion on occasions.

Ribbon Loop Garter: Worn around 1660, ribbon loop garters finished off Trousers – see **slops**. They were decorative loops of ribbon.

Fringed Sash Garter: They have the same use as a ribbon loop garter but were probably worn earlier, around 1640.

Sports Socks: Thick, knitted socks for use in outdoor sports to protect the feet and lower legs and keep them warm.

Cod Piece: A small bag or box that concealed the front opening of a man's breeches and often contained kerchiefs and money.

Bobby Sock (US)/Ankle Sock: Knitted socks that finished at the ankle. Bobby socks were thicker and were rolled down and worn with sneakers by American teenagers.

Leg Warmers: Neoprene™ leg warmers shaped to fit the legs and keep them warm, during sporting activities.

Tube Socks: Simple knitted socks, in the shape of a tube, fitting all sizes and very cheap to manufacture but liable to wear at the heel.

Clocks: These are ornamental designs embroidered or woven on to the ankles of stockings, they were meant to draw attention to a pretty ankle.

Edwardian Stocking: Highly decorative stockings held up with garters or suspenders ensuring that no part of the leg was visible.

Hold Up: As the stocking, but the hold up may or may not be seamed. A permanently sticky cuff is enough to hold the stocking in place and is disguised by lace. The sticky substance is not spoiled by laundering.

Fall Down/Roll Down: This sock can be knitted or woven and is meant to hang baggily away from the leg around the ankle.

Japanese Cotton Sock: A Japanese sock with a sole that has a division for the first toe, the other four are compartmentalised together.

Leg Warmers (Knitted): Footless knitted legs that reach to the knees, these are worn by dancers to keep their legs warm during rehearsals and any physical activity. They wrap slightly under the foot and then wrinkle around the ankle.

Arm Warmers: As the neoprene leg warmers but for the arms, these are very useful to cyclists.

Knee Warmers: As the neoprene leg warmers and arm warmers.

Suspender Belt: A stretch fabric garment with suspender clips to attach stockings.

Sleeve Bands: Springy metal sleeve bands are used to control shirt sleeves and are worn on the upper arm.

Sleeve Clips: These form a similar function to the sleeve bands, except that they clip fabric in lumps wherever it is required. They are a useful styling tool.

Belt with Cords and Clips: The clips were used to hitch up long skirts when walking, from the eighteenth to the early twentieth century.

Suspender Belt (Straight Front): As the suspender belt, here the stockings fasten at the front only.

Suspenders (US)/Braces: These have been used from the late eighteenth century to support trousers when a belt is not being worn. They are nowadays elasticated and attach to the trousers using buttons on metal clips. (Also known as gallouses).

PRODUCTION

Seams
Page 166

Flatlock Seam: The type of seam most frequently used, where the two edges to be sewn together are joined and pressed open and flat. Depending on the fabric used the seam allowance starts around 1 cm.

Zig-zagged Seam: A zig-zagged stitch is used instead of a straight stitch. This is to allow for a certain amount of stretch when using a knitted fabric.

Piping: A cord, thick or thin depending on the weight of the fabric and desired effect, is sandwiched in a binding and then set into a seam. It makes the seam less flexible and is better used on straight or slightly curved seams or hem edges.

Weighted Hem with Lead Discs: Small lead discs are applied to' the inside of the garment, on seams, so that they are not visible from the right side. Their function is to pull the seams straight and weight hems to allow them to hang as the designer intended.

Superlock Seam: This seam involves two processes in one. The superlock machine stitches the seam as a flatlock seam and overlocks to neaten the seam at the same time. The seam allowance only needs to be 0.75 cm.

Stitched and Pinked Seam: A flatlock stitched seam that is finished by using pinking shears. Used on heavyweight fabrics that are less likely to fray.

Binding: A decorative edging using self-fabric or a contrasting fabric where a conventional hem or facing is not desired.

Herringbone Stitch: A strong hemming stitch for heavier fabrics.

Flatlock and Overlocked Together: A normal flatlock seam but the two edges are overlocked together and pressed to one side.

Run and Fell Seam: The seam is made on the right side of the garment. A normal seam is created and stitched using 1.5 cm seam allowance (depending on the fabric). One side is trimmed, the other is turned over it and pressed under 0.5 cm and the whole seam is then topstitched on the right side. These seams are typically used in jeans and denim clothing.

Slot Seam: Another piece of fabric, probably contrasting, is introduced into this seam, so that part of the contrast is visible, it is then topstitched into place.

Hem with Mitred Corner: For square hems and edges, the turn-back of the hem is mitred at the corner for a good finish, getting rid of any surplus fabric.

Exposed Seam: The stitching is shown on the right side of the garment. Here it is made with a Rimoldi machine, used in manufacturing underwear, lightweight knitted garments and jersey and Lycra™ garments. The effect is that of stitching and neatening the seam with a series of needles that spread across the seam.

Mock Run and Fell: This has the same appearance as the run and fell seam from the right side, but the seam is constructed like a flatlocked and overlocked seam, pressed to one side and then topstitched on the right side.

Faggoting: A decorative finish between two pieces of material. It is a series of criss-cross stitches from one edge to another that shows an open area between them.

Weighted Hem with Lead Pellets: See **weighted hem with lead discs**. Here, the weight is given by a string of lead pellets.

Rimoldi Seam: See **exposed seam**.

Fur Seam: Skins are laid together and stitched on the edge with specialist machinery.

Boning/Stay Strip: Boning is a flexible plastic strip that is used to emphasise and support shape in evening wear, dance wear etc. The boning is laid on the seam with strips of fabric laid and stitched over it, to protect the wearer.

Weighted Hem with Chain Chanel Style: See **weighted hem with lead discs**. Here the weight is from a chain applied to the hem, attributed to the designer Coco Chanel.

French Seam: A seam used in manufacture with sheer, lightweight fabrics. The seam is constructed by making a normal seam of around 0.5 cm on the right side of the garment. This is then trimmed and pressed and turned to the wrong side where another 0.5 cm seam allowance is taken which sandwiches all raw edges within it.

Lace Seam: The lace fabric is overlapped following its own pattern as much as possible. This is then overstitched on one edge and the other edge is trimmed away.

Taped Seam: Used on curved seams, the tape strengthens the seam and stops the fabric stretching.

Intersecting/Crossed Seam: A series of flatlock seams in contrasting fabric creating a regular patchwork effect.

Finishes
Page 167

Piccadills: This is the scalloped or tabbed edge of a garment at the neck, armhole or waist, popular in the late sixteenth and seventeenth centuries. The name is thought to be derived from a tailor who specialised in such finishes, and resided in Piccadilly Hall in St Martin-in-the-Fields.

Couching: Decorative cords or braids are laid on the surface of a garment and are then stitched in place.

Drawn Thread Work: Threads are pulled from the warp or weft of a fabric and trimmed and finished to create decorative open spaces.

Blanket Stitch: An edge stitching to neaten bulky fabrics like woollen blanketing that are impossible to turn back and hem. It can be used as a decorative as well as a practical finish.

Gusset: A triangular piece of fabric set into a garment to create an enlarged area, for ease of movement or to strengthen the garment (see sleeves, **dolman with gusset** and the **slavian** trouser).

Trapunto: Decorative machine stitch following a pattern. Sometimes the pattern is accentuated by piping cord, or padding of any sort, laid under the garment and covered with a backing for neatness.

Flounce: A circular cut frill set into a seam or at a hem, very like ruffles.

Elastic Webbing: A strongly woven strip with elastic content that stretches and can be used in waistbands to draw up fabric, and wherever else strength is needed. Simple dirndl skirts can be made this way and fabric is available with the webbing already in place.

Handmade Eyelet: Regularly made holes in fabric that are finished with decorative stitching.

Wadded Quilting: Regular but decorative stitches on fabric to keep wadding in place. The wadding adds extra warmth to a garment and is sandwiched between the actual garment fabric and a backing fabric.

Gallant: Originating from the seventeenth century, this was a form of decoration adopted by men and women, but mostly men. It involved ribbon loops and bows that were applied in abundance all over the garments.

Belt Loops/Carriers: Small straps fitted into waistbands to carry belts. They can also be discreet crocheted loops that are hardly visible.

Slashing: See **slashed trunk hose** for a full description of the origins of slashing. A regular decorative feature of the sixteenth century.

Fringing: A garment may be finished by removing weft threads to form a fringe which can then be stay-stitched to prevent it unravelling further. The garment edge must be straight to achieve satisfactory results. A fringe can also be made in a contrasting fabric and applied where needed or commercial fringing may be used.

Knitted Rib: Used to finish knitted garments such as sweatshirts. The neck edge, waistline and cuffs may be finished in this way. It gives a snug and practical fit to the garment.

Smocking (Honeycomb Stitch): A decorative method of controlling fullness – the garment is stitched in a variety of stitches, here with a honeycomb stitch. It is an ancient practice but is still popular on children's clothes and occasionally in fashion.

Dagges: A medieval form of decoration from the fourteenth to the fifteenth centuries, the edges of a garment were cut into regular jagged shapes. This decoration appeared on all kinds of garments. See also **piccadills**.

Casing with Drawstring: A piece of fabric with a self-casing is drawn up with a drawstring so that fit is adjustable.

Pleated Frill: A decorative trim that consists of tiny pleats fixed on a binding and used to finish garments.

Machine Embroidery: Sewing machines nowadays are very versatile and capable of many varieties of decorative stitching.

Dagges: Another version of dagged edges. See **dagges** earlier for a full description.

Fitchet: A vertical opening on the hip of a gown or surcoat to allow the hand to be padded through to the purse or belt worn inside for security. It is a medieval term.

Turn-up: A decorative finish to skirts, trousers or cuffs, designed so that the face of the fabric still shows.

Scalloped Edge: A regular, curved shape cut into hems and edges as a decorative finish, not so deeply cut as a dagged edge. The decorative edge would be faced or overstitched to neaten it.

Picot Edge: A much smaller version of the scalloped edge, normally finished with an overstitch as opposed to a facing.

Fullness
Page 168

Square Yoke: The bodice is split into two straight across the back or front of a garment using a variety of proportions. It allows contrasting fabrics and other methods of creative construction to be used.

Sunray Pleats: Pleats from a central point that radiate out to the edge of the garment.

Top-stitched Pleats: Any kind of pleat, but part of the pleat is top-stitched to create a fixed shape that then contrasts with the unstitched pleat.

Elastication: Fabric that is drawn up with elastic so that it is flexible rather than fixed (see **peasant blouse**).

Watteau Pleats: Pleats at the back of a gown, known as the Robe à la Française. The pleats are known as Watteau pleats and are stitched down at the back of the neckline and then allowed to fall freely to the ground.

Casing with Heading: A piece of fabric is drawn up with a drawstring or elastic held in a tunnel made by applying a strip of fabric to the surface leaving a border at the top or bottom for decoration.

Knife Pleats: Pleats of any width similar to accordion pleats, but all face the same direction when folded.

Accordion Pleats: Very narrow, straight pleats, equal in width to each other.

Pin Tucks: Tiny lines of pleats that are stitched down. They can be any distance apart and are purely decorative. They are seen on shirts, blouses, skirts etc., usually on lightweight fabrics.

Unpressed Pleats: Any kind of pleat that has not been pressed. They have a rounded appearance.

Self-casing: A piece of fabric where the hem edge is folded over and neatened to create a tunnel. A drawstring or elastic is then threaded through the tunnel to draw up the fabric.

One-Piece Facing/Extended Facing/Self-facing: A finished edge is created by extending part of a garment, using the front and mirroring the actual garment. This extended piece is folded back to neaten and reinforce the garment.

Ruffles: Strips of fabric cut from circles and then opened out and applied inside a band or on a seam. They can be of any width, but may need to be seamed together to create a long ruffle.

Kick Pleat: A small pleat placed in a garment to allow more movement, usually in a tight skirt.

Box Pleats: The fabric is folded equally on both sides and the edges of the pleat meet at the centre of the back of the pleat.

Storm Flap/Cape Yoke: The top part of this construction echoes the shape underneath but flare is added to create the cape effect. This part is then laid over the original shape. The storm flap has less flare and simply provides an extra layer of protection during poor weather – found on rainwear and protective garments.

Reinforced Inverted Pleat: As the inverted pleat, but with the addition of reinforcements to keep the pleat in a certain position.

Inverted Pleat: A single reversed box pleat where the pleat is not seen from the front, just the two edges meeting together.

Shirring: Fabric is drawn up to create fullness using a fine elasticated thread known as shirring elastic. It can be used in a series of lines, depending on the effect required.

Shaped Facing: A garment is finished with a piece of fabric, with seam allowance, that mirrors the garment shape. This example shows the inside of an armhole.

Wired Hem: The hem provides a tunnel through which wire can be threaded. The wire can be light and flexible, forming slight flutes, or it can be firmer, giving the effect of a steel hoop.

Crystal Pleats: Very fine pleats like accordion pleats but much smaller.

Tab: A bagged out piece of fabric that is buttoned or studded in place. It can be used on pockets and fastenings or to control fullness.

Tucked Yoke: As the square yoke but a pleat or tuck has been added horizontally and top-stitched down.

Ruching: Fabric is drawn up with a thread or drawstring to create a full, gathered effect within a garment.

Elastic in a Casing: A piece of fabric is drawn up with elastic through a casing. See **self-casing**.

Gathers: Fabric is drawn up, arranged and fixed within a flat band.

Gun Patch: A reinforced patch is placed on the shoulder – here for protection when shooting.

Flange Dart: A dart that is only partly stitched, the rest of it being laid free rather like a pleat. This example shows an armhole with flange dart.

Gathering Threads: Either done by hand or else the longest stitch on a sewing machine is used with the tension suitably adjusted. Two rows of stitching are run through a piece of fabric, then the threads are drawn up to create gathers.

Gathered Frill: A narrow, straight piece of cloth is drawn up and fixed within a seam or at the hem of a garment to create a decorative finish.

Yoke with Pocket: This pocket is like the epaulette pocket. It is set into the yoke seam.

Pockets
Page 169

Patch: A pocket that is pressed and sewn on to the exterior of a garment.

Patch with Pleat: As the patch pocket, but with a box pleat to create more space within the pocket.

Jetted: The pocket is constructed by cutting through the garment to the required length of the finished pocket, then the edges are bound and a pocket bag attached to the back of the garment.

Jetted with Reinforcement: As the jetted pocket, but with leather or fabric patches stitched to the edge of the pocket to strengthen the finished binding.

Bound Patch: As the patch pocket but here shown gathered into a binding applied to the top edge to neaten it.

Shirt: Normally a breast pocket placed on any kind of shirt but usually a work shirt. It is a patch pocket with a shaped bottom and a turned back and top-stitched welt effect at the top.

Patch with Flap: As the patch pocket but with a bagged out flap, the same width as the patch and stitched above the patch, to cover the opening. It is finished with a button or stud fastening.

Welt: Similar in construction to the jetted pocket in that the garment is slashed to the length of the finished pocket and a folded and bagged out piece of fabric, the width of the finished pocket, plus seam allowance, is set into the slash and stitched up at the sides. The extended flap is stitched down at the sides and covers the pocket opening.

Jetted with Zip: As the jetted pocket but with a zip set into the opening created by the bindings.

Shirred Patch: As the patch pocket but the head of the pocket is elasticated to create a more spacious pocket.

Double Pocket: This is a patch pocket that is layered to create two pockets. The zipped top is the entrance to one pocket and here the left side is the entry for the other.

Post Box in Patch: The patch pocket and jetted pocket combined in that the entrance to the pocket is through the jet, the patch being stitched all the way round.

Angled Flap: A shaped flap set into the garment like an upside down welt.

Jetted with Tab: As the jetted pocket but with a tab for fastening set into the jet.

Mechanic's: Normally seen on dungarees, overalls and work jeans, the mechanic's pocket is a large patch with cut away top and tag at the bottom for hanging tools.

Utility: Like the kangaroo pocket but with many more divisions for specific tools and instruments.

Western: Like the angled flap but with a bottom curving to a point, echoing the Western or cowboy style of pocket.

Jetted with Flap: This pocket is like the jet with tab. The flap runs the full width of the pocket and here has curved corners.

Bellows: A patch pocket with a pleat set behind it that expands to accommodate articles placed within it. Applied to work jackets and coats.

Patch with Tab: As the patch pocket but with an extended tab and button head for decoration only.

Denim Top-Stitched: A patch pocket made from denim and applied to denim jeans and other jeans-styled garments. It has the hallmark twin top-stitching.

Rounded Flap: Like the angled flap but with curved edges.

Curved Jet: As the jetted pocket but the cut in the garment is curved, not straight. This example has leather reinforcements.

Bucket: A patch pocket cut with flare at the top, like a cowl neck, and applied to the external surface of the garment. It creates a draped silhouette.

Petal: A patch pocket that is split in two and overlapped with a curved top, to created a folded petal effect.

Kangaroo: A wide patch pocket split into two by a stitch line.

Contoured Jet with Reinforcement: As the curved jet but the opening is exaggerated to show the pocket bag, which is made in a contrast fabric. The corners are also reinforced.

Hidden in Seam: This pocket has the appearance of the curved jet, but is much simpler in construction. It is set into a seam, topstitched and reinforced, pocket bags are applied to the seam allowance inside the garment.

Epaulette Pocket: This pocket is similar to the hidden in seam pocket, the seam being part of a raglan sleeve and set close to the shoulder. Consequently the pocket has the name epaulette, i.e. shoulder ornament.

Side: This pocket is set into the side seam of a garment, similar to the hidden in seam pocket.

Curved Inset: The pocket here is constructed as part of the front of the trouser or skirt, the back of the pocket is also part of the construction. The back of the pocket bag is an extension of that part of the garment, the front of it is effectively a facing to the front part of the garment.

Slanted Inset: As the curved inset but the shape of the pocket is that of a slant instead of a curve.

Cargo: Similar in construction to the mechanic's pocket but applied to the waist of jeans or dungarees. The belt passes through the top of the pocket.

Ticket: Introduced to carry railways tickets around 1860, the ticket pocket is frequently seen on denim jeans.

Fastenings
Page 170
Studded Placket (Wet Weather): A placket that covers a conventional fastening for extra protection in wet weather.

Four- and Two-hole Sew-through Buttons: Two buttons with four and two holes which can be of any size and used on any type of garment.

Hook and Eye: Can be used as discreet fastenings like the press-stud fastener.

Frog Fastening: A looped fastening of braid or cord, worn on military and oriental garments. Depending on fashion it can be used in many other circumstances.

Woman's Fastening: The opposite of the man's fastening. The garment is wrapped over the left-hand side with buttonholes on the right and buttons on the left.

Toggle Fastening: A frog-type fastening made from cord and fastened with a toggle, made from wood or plastic. Seen on duffle coats.

Ratchet Spring and Hook: A metal or plastic fastening used mainly on luggage.

Man's Fastening: The garment is wrapped over the right-hand side with buttonholes on the left and buttons on the right.

Reinforced Button: A very small button is set behind the main button and the placket to reinforce the fabric against the pull of the main button. It is used on heavy coats and jackets.

Tailored Buttonholes: Shaped buttonholes with a small hole at the end of the cut for the button to sit comfortably when fastened.

Zip with Guard: A zip fastening with guard behind, to protect the wearer, found on jackets and on fly fronts.

Self-shank Button: There are no sew-through holes to attach the button, but a shank at the base which is part of the button.

Rouleau Loops: Strips of fabric stitched and pressed to form loops for fastening buttons. They are usually set at the edge of a placket.

Popper/Press Stud/Snap Fastening (US): Studs with holes to sew through and attach to a garment. They are normally used where a fastening should be invisible. They snap together easily and can be made from metal or plastic.

Zip and Stud (Double Fastening): A double fastening of zip and studded placket, for wet weather protection. The studs are backed for re-inforcement. Here the zip opens from the bottom as well as the top for access to internal pockets in cold weather without undoing the whole coat.

Metal Shank: As the self-shank button but here the base is made from a metal loop that is attached to the button.

Covered Button: A metal or plastic button that allows the designer to cover it with any fabric. It has a clip base that snaps into place for a tidy finish. The buttons are available in a variety of sizes and are popular on multi-button fastening wedding dresses, etc.

Snap Tape: A set of studs is applied to tape, the opposite sides being attached to another tape. It is the tapes that are stitched in place.

Asymmetrical Fastening: A wrap-over fastening that is developed from the double-breasted fastening. The wrap-over can be shaped.

Fur Tack: A round tack that clips together to fasten and is used primarily on fur coats.

Velcro™: A unique fastening system in which one side is made up of tiny hooks repeated across the surface while the other side is of softer, fluffy construction on which the hooks cling. This forms a very secure fastening, but one which can be easily pulled apart. It is used for clothes, footwear, nappies and display systems. It is particularly suited to children and the arthritic elderly where the fine control for dealing with buttons or zips is lacking.

In-seam Buttonhole: The seam is left open the length of the button, to allow the button to pass through.

Hook and Eye Fastening: Metal hooks and eyes can also be used as an alternative fastening to buttons. The hooks and eyes need a placket behind them to form a pleasing fastening.

Page 171

Gimp Covered Fur Hook and Eye: A hook and eye for use on fur garments, covered in silk, wool or metal thread, known as gimp, for a more luxurious feel.

Button Placket (Topstitched): Topstitching is both decorative and practical in that it can highlight detail but also reinforce the garment.

Dog Clip: A metal clip seen on dog leads but also used in garments and on belts and accessories.

Reversible Zip: A zip with two pullers so that a garment can be made reversible. Can be metal or chunky plastic.

Cord Loop: A corded loop that can be set into a seam for fastening buttons – a similar function to the rouleau loop.

Brace/Suspender Clip: A metal or plastic clip used to fasten braces or suspenders.

Hook and Bar: A flat metal fastening, one side hooks on to the other, often used on waistbands.

Hook and Eye (Strip): Like the previous versions of the hook and eye but here placed in strips for use in underwear and corsetry.

Thread Loop: This is like the cord loop but here it is made from crocheting the loop into the seam.

Bra Hook/Swimsuit Hook: A metal or plastic hook that interlocks and is used on swimwear and underwear.

Overall Adjuster and Buckle: Primarily used on dungarees for adults and children. It can be made from metal or plastic but needs to be strong. The adjuster allows for a perfect fit in adults and for extending in children to adapt for growth. The shaped buckle loops over a shanked button.

Anchor Buckle: An interlocking fastening shaped like an anchor, for use on accessories, swimwear or underwear.

Commercial Braid/Soutache: A commercially made braid that is made from matt or shiny fibres. It can be used as decorative loop fastenings or couched and stitched on the surface of garments.

D-Rings: Loops of metal that allow fabric ties to be passed through and back over themselves to fasten.

Interlocking Fastener: Metal fastenings that interlock tightly when some tension is applied, as with elasticated belts.

Tassel: Widely used in all kinds of garments and accessories, the tassel is a yarn fringe which is rolled up and held together with a covered knob at the top. It may be made in a variety of yarns and threads and can be used as a functional fastening in conjunction with a large cord loop.

Man's Fly Front with French Bearer: A man's fly front fastening with placket guard and French bearer. The French bearer is a button tab that passes under the fastening, to button on the inside of the garment, to allow for a good fit in men's tailored trousers.

Buckles: Buckles can be bought in a variety of shapes and sizes and are used on accessories – bags, belts, etc.

Tie Fastening: Made from fabric and can be used anywhere.

Knot: A method of fastening and decoration used throughout history. Knots can be used on virtually any part of a garment.

Fly Front (Closed): A strong zip fastener applied to trousers, jeans and skirts. The zip is hidden under the placket on the left and sandwiched between the placket and the guard on the right side.

Metal Eyelet: Metal eyelets can be applied to most fabrics but require some reinforcement on the reverse of a garment. They are ideal for lacing garments.

Lacing: Cords or ties are passed through holes or looped eyelets to form a laced fastening. Lacing can also be purely decorative combined with another method of fastening.

Bows: Bows can be functional fastenings or purely decorative and applied wherever required.

CONSTRUCTION

Sleeves
Page 172

Set in: The sleeve is shaped around the arm and has a seam on the underarm. The top of the sleeve, the sleeve head, is curved to accommodate the roundness of the shoulder. The sleeve is constructed and then 'set into' the bodice.

Bracelet/Three-quarter: This sleeve reaches halfway between the elbow and the wrist.

Padded Shoulder: The shoulder is extended and the sleeve is heightened to accommodate a pad to achieve a squared or rounded effect in the silhouette.

Raglan with Yoke: See **raglan with dart**. Here the raglan is extended to accommodate the top part of the bodice, achieving a 'yoke' effect. There is a seam along the top edge of the sleeve and at the underarm.

Dropped Shoulder: The shoulder is extended and shaped around the shoulder, rather like the capped sleeve. However, there is more shaping and the extension is usually longer; also a sleeve is actually set into the armhole. The sleeve construction is modified by removing that part of the head that is now covered by the extension to the shoulder. The sleeve head then looks less curved.

Man's Shirt: A set-in sleeve with two pleats at the buttoned cuff and a placket. Normally seen on men's shirts.

Two-piece Tailored: A shaped sleeve that has a seam down the front and the back to allow for shaping. There is no underarm seam, consequently the sleeve is constructed in two pieces.

Saddle Raglan: See **raglan with dart**. Here the seam for applying the sleeve to the bodice is shaped, it narrows along the shoulder line. This sleeve has a seam at the underarm and along the top edge of the arm to the wrist, including the shoulder.

Raglan with Dart: The raglan sleeve is derived from the set-in sleeve but with the shoulder added to the sleeve head. It was named after Lord Raglan who led the Charge of the Light Brigade in the Crimean War and wore raglan sleeved jackets. The sleeve is cut in one piece but has a dart at the shoulder to accommodate the shoulder.

Raglan with Seam: A normal raglan shaped sleeve with a seam along the top edge of the arm, and at the underarm. See **raglan with dart**.

Capped (Extended Shoulder): This is an extension of the shoulder just covering the shoulder point.

Capped: The sleeve is an insertion that just covers the shoulder point.

Bell: Like the long bell sleeve, but much shorter, finishing around elbow length.

Wing Ruffle: Like the capped sleeve but here the fabric extension has fullness added, the fabric being gathered and set onto the bodice creating a ruffle effect.

Cape: A full, flared sleeve that is set into the armhole. The sleeve could be cut as a circle to give more flare at the hem.

Frill: The upper part of the sleeve fits the arm, the lower part has a deep, gathered frill at about elbow length.

Long Bell: The upper part of the sleeve fits the arm, the lower part flares out into a full, bell shape.

Bishop: The reverse of the leg of mutton – the top part is fitted and then flares out towards the wrist where the sleeve is gathered onto a cuff. A popular 1960s style.

Pagoda: An eighteenth century sleeve, fitted on the upper arm, with tiered frills on the lower part of the arm to the wrist. It can be longer at the back of the wrist. There are usually three tiers giving the appearance of a Chinese pagoda.

Page 173

Leg of Mutton: A full, gathered sleeve head is set into the bodice and the long sleeve tapers to fit towards the wrist. Popular in the late nineteenth and early twentieth century, fashion frequently reintroduces the leg of mutton.

Juliet: A two-part sleeve similar in effect to the leg of mutton. The top part of the sleeve is full and gathered while the lower part of the sleeve is fitted to the arm and is seamed to the top part above the elbow.

Melon/Balloon: A very full, short set-in sleeve, padded out to give the effect of a melon or balloon.

Puffed: A set-in sleeve that has fullness at the sleeve head and base. It is set into the bodice and controlled at the base by a cuff or elastication to give a 'puffed' effect.

Peasant: A full, short sleeve that is attached to a full bodice with a raglan effect seam. The garment is drawn in with elastic or a drawstring to the neck and at the sleeve hem. There are many variations to this theme.

Lantern: A long set-in sleeve constructed in two parts. The top part flares slightly from the sleeve head towards the wrist. The bottom part flares from a fitting wrist to meet the flare of the top. Both are seamed together a few inches above the wrist.

Short Lantern: The same principle as the lantern, but a much shorter version ending just past the elbow.

Double: A puffed sleeve with two layers – the base is opaque and the top sleeve is transparent to reveal the sleeve underneath.

Drawstring Puffed: A full sleeve, short or long, with a drawstring to draw the sleeve to the desired size. The drawing up forms a small frill at the hem of the sleeve. Here the head is not gathered (see also **puffed**).

Petal/Lapped: This sleeve is cut without an underarm seam and is shaped and folded on the upper arm. It was very popular in the 1940s.

Mamaluke/Virago: A long, full sleeve, that is partitioned into five, full sections. The five sleeve parts are drawn and seamed together to fit around the arm.

Draped: A set-in sleeve that is slashed open at the top part of the sleeve where fullness is added; the underarm seam remains the original length. The extra fullness created is drawn up with a drawstring or elastic to fix it into place, creating a 'draped' effect.

Dolman/Magyar: This style is named from the Magyars in Hungary and was worn by peasants there. The shoulder seam extends through the top of the sleeve and the underarm seam follows from the side of the bodice through to the wrist. There are no other seams and any shaping is made from these two.

Square Armhole: The armhole is shaped like a square with a right angle at the corner. The construction is as a set-in sleeve.

Strapped/Banded: The construction is that of a set-in sleeve. From the neck point to the wrist is a narrow band of fabric giving a strapped effect.

Epaulette and Elbow Patch: A strap or tab on the shoulder, normally seen on uniforms, to carry caps. Here there is also a patch on the elbow to protect the garment and prolong its life in heavy-duty use.

Dolman with Gusset: See **dolman/Magyar**. This sleeve has a gusset set under the arm to allow for more 'lift'.

Kimono: A long sleeve that is a complete extension of the bodice to the wrist. The seam lines are along the top of the sleeve and at the underarm. A traditionally Japanese sleeve used on the garment with the same name.

Page 174

Batwing: The same principle as the kimono. This sleeve narrows towards the wrist and has a curved underarm seam. This particular example would be made from a knitted fabric.

Dalmatian/Angel: A sleeve that flares towards the wrist extending into a long point.

Bag: A long and very full sleeve that is gathered onto the cuff at the wrist. It has the effect of bagging on the lower part of the arm. This sleeve was popular in the fifteenth and sixteenth centuries.

Tippet on Elbow: Popular in the Middle Ages. This was a pendant effect hanging from the elbow of a gown or tunic. It was similar in derivation to the liripipe.

Slashed Virago: See **mamaluke/virago** (p.173): This sleeve has the upper part incorporating slashing, a popular sixteenth century decorative effect. The slashing reveals the shirt or tunic underneath, giving a contrast. Here there is extra contrast with the lower part of the sleeve being constructed in a different colour or fabric.

Trailing Sleeve: This is similar to the hanging sleeve. The sleeve is constructed like a kimono and the opening for the hand is in the same position while the bottom part of the sleeve is stitched up.

Cartwheel/Circle: A short, set-in sleeve, designed to give an accordion effect.

Buttoned Oversleeve: A medieval sleeve that has a contrasting sleeve layered over the base sleeve. The top sleeve can be unbuttoned to reveal the contrast beneath.

Hanging: This is a very long sleeve that is open down the front seam and hangs vertically. It is part of a medieval gown or doublet.

Mahoitres: A fourteenth and fifteenth century sleeve popular in France. The sleeve is padded and bag shaped.

Cuffs
Page 175

Faced Hem: A simple finish to a sleeve where the hem is faced and topstitched.

Shaped Faced Hem: The same as the faced hem but here a notch is included.

Faced Placket: The sleeve has a cuff added and the slit up the sleeve (the placket) allows it to pass over the hand. This is faced and topstitched.

Man's Tailored Shirt: The placket is visible on the right side of the shirt and neatens and strengthens the slit in the sleeve.

Loose Pleat Cuff: Here the slit is faced, shaped and topstitched and works when the cuff is buttoned.

Angled: The cuff is shaped and applied as normal to the sleeve.

Curved: As the angled cuff but here the shape is that of a curve.

Turn Back: The cuff is quite long and here has a three-button fastening. The edge of it has a turn-up. When a cuff is quite deep or long the relative length must be removed from the sleeve to allow for this.

Turn-up: Here there is no cuff and the turn-up is continuous all the way round the hem.

French Cuff with Cuff Links: A cuff design like a **turn back** the full depth of the cuff. The cuff usually needs to be secured with cuff links on a chain or shank rather than buttons.

Long Fitted: A long cuff that is shaped to fit the arm. This example has a multi-button fastening.

Button Tab: A sleeve without a cuff that is faced and has the addition of an adjustable tab for fit.

Gauntlet: When a cuff is deeper than 3 inches (7.6 cm) it is known as a gauntlet. Here the cuff turns back and has many buttons to fasten it. The turn back must increase in width as it leads up the arm.

Western: A shaped and braided or top-stitched cuff – reminiscent of the decoration on costumes worn by American Country and Western singers and also cowboys.

Tramline/Top-Stitched: A faced sleeve that has multiple lines of topstitching for decoration.

Rouleau Loop: A faced sleeve hem with a faced slit. The fastening is that of many button-through rouleau loops. See PRODUCTION – **rouleau loops**.

Button Vent: Used in a tailored sleeve, there is a vent which is fixed with buttons. They may be false buttons without holes, for decoration only.

Button Extension: A button-holed extension is added to the sleeve and wraps over the sleeve to fasten.

Zipped: A zip is inserted into what would have been the placket slit.

Bound: The slit is left open but is finished by binding along the hem and around the slit.

Wedge Inset: A wedge of fabric is inserted into the slit to allow for fit over the hand and for its decorative quality.

Fringed: The hem is finished with a decorative fringe.

Elasticated Cuff: A full sleeve hem with self-casing is controlled by elastication for a good fit.

Buckle and Strap: A full sleeve hem is controlled here with a strap and buckle-fastener.

Elasticated with Frill: As with the **elasticated cuff** but here there is also a frill created.

Ruched: The sleeve hem has been extended and is then secured back into position with a line of gathering or ruching to create a draped effect.

Placket with Gathers: The slit in the sleeve, and the sleeve length, is extended and controlled by gathering the fullness back up and finishing it with a shaped placket.

Drawstring: Like the **elasticated cuff**, but here the fullness is controlled by an adjustable drawstring.

Ribbed/Knitted: The fullness of a knitted fabric sleeve is controlled by a ribbed, knitted cuff that hugs the wrist.

Collars
Page 176

Straight Band: A strip of fabric encircling the neck.

Bateau: A straight band placed on a wide neckline.

Ring: A band of fabric that is shaped in toward the neck.

Polo/Turtle/Roll: A wide piece of fabric, usually knitted or cut on the cross, that folds back to form a roll neck collar.

Mandarin/Nehru: An Oriental collar that is a straight band, but that opens at the front and has curved edges. Also popular in India but generally the edges are straight rather than curved. See also Tops – **mandarin** and Jackets – **Nehru**.

Peter Pan: A flat, curved shaped collar with no stand.

Asymmetrical Straight Band: A straight band of fabric with the fastening on one side. There is a placket supporting the button fastening.

Cossack: A narrow band around the neck that is fastened on one side. It is similar to the asymmetrical straight band.

Bishop: A shirt-type collar with points extending into tab shapes and no fastening down the front.

Tab: A straight band with one of the fronts extending into a placket effect for access.

Convertible Closed: See **convertible open**. When closed the convertible collar is similar in appearance to the shirt collar with stand.

Convertible Open: A straight, pointed collar, which can be worn open or closed. The top collar is cut in one with the facing. There is only one seam at the back of the neck. It is seen most frequently on shirts or blouses.

Shirt Collar with Stand Tailored: A fold-over collar supported by a stiffened stand. It has a neat, tailored effect.

Button Down: A fold-over collar usually on a stand where the points are buttoned down onto the body of the shirt as a decorative feature.

Giraffe: A very high collar on a deep stand with a two-button fastening. The collar turns down and has rounded fronts.

Danton: A high-necked collar with deep fold over.

Napoleon High Coat/Highwayman/High Fold: A high, turned down collar, sometimes even rising above the ears, as worn by Napoleon and often seen on coats and jackets of his time.

Wing Tipped: A stiffened straight band that has a fastening at the front, the edges of the collar are folded over to give a wing effect. Generally worn with formal wear.

Shawl: A long, roll-back collar that follows the line of a jacket or coat that is cut as a 'V' and then wraps over to fasten. There is a seam at the back neck.

Revers: The rever is formed by the folding back of the lapel. The lapel is faced to form the top collar, the under collar on the lapel being an extension of the body of the garment. The top and bottom collars that wrap around the neck are two separate pieces.

Clover Revers: See **fishmouth revers**. Here the edges of the lapels are curved.

Tuxedo: Similar to the shawl collar, but here longer and usually made from a contrast satin or silk for use on evening wear. See also **tuxedo** further on in this section and Jackets – **tuxedo**.

Fishmouth Revers: Shaped revers resembling a fish mouth.

Shaped Shawl: As the shawl collar but here with a notch cut out to create shaping.

Italian: Similar to the convertible collar and popular in Italy on suits.

L-Revers: See **fishmouth revers** but here the shape is that of an 'L'.

Chelsea: A V-shaped neck with a straight collar set in that meets at the front.

Portrait: A wide neckline supporting a fold-over collar that overlaps at the front.

Sailor: A V-shaped neckline with a collar similar to the Chelsea but with a deep, cape-like, square back, usually trimmed with contrasting braid.

Puritan: A simple but deep, fold-over collar as worn by the Puritans of the seventeenth century.

Round Bertha: A cape-like collar that usually covered the shoulders. It was generally made from lace and was popular in the nineteenth and early twentieth centuries.

Page 177

Square Bertha: As the round bertha, except that here the cape collar is squared off.

Dutch: A double layered cape-like collar, popular in Holland.

Pierrot: A soft collar, cut as a circle for maximum fullness, as worn by the European clown known as Pierrot. Often revived in fashion. See also **Pierrot top**.

Ruff: A stiffened, pleated collar popular in the sixteenth century.

Falling Band: A term meaning a soft, unstiffened collar that draped over the shoulders, popular in the seventeenth century.

Vandyke: Similar to the standing band and made of lace, it features in the paintings by Van Dyck.

Gorget: A collar covering the throat and the neck and usually made in linen. Popular in the fourteenth century.

Partlet: A high collar for framing the face. It was stiffened and made in lace and worn in the late sixteenth century.

Standing Band: The opposite of the falling band, popular at the same time, a high neck collar that framed the face.

Barbette: A linen band that covered the neck and chin of a woman which was popular from the thirteenth to the sixteenth century. This medieval style is preserved, together with the wimple, in the clothing of some nuns.

Carcaille: A built up neckline from the late fourteenth century. This example has a fur trim.

Cascade/Jabot: A frill or ruffle attached to the front of a garment, it decreases in size towards the base.

Modesty Piece: A piece of lace or ribbon attached to the top of a corset to act as a 'fill in' on gowns with low necklines. A popular eighteenth and nineteenth century fashion.

Ascot: A soft collar that has extended ties for fastening. See also **Ascot** in ACCESSORIES – Neckwear.

Bow/Tie: Like the Ascot but tied in a soft bow.

Central Stitched Ruffle: A central placket front with ruffle trim around the edges.

Bib with Frill: A bib-shaped front with a frill trim.

Tuxedo: A rolled collar that is the same width extending right down the front edges of a coat or jacket. See also **tuxedo** earlier in this section.

Eton: A stiff, white collar turned down and emulating those worn by boys at Eton College.

Betsie: A stiff collar or ruff worn around the neck as epitomised by Elizabeth I.

Collarette with Décolleté: A band of fabric such as lace or velvet that is gathered up and worn around a woman's neck. Worn in the sixteenth to eighteenth century with décolleté or low necklines. See Necklines – **décolleté** for a slightly different design.

Canezou: A cape-like garment made in a transparent fabric and trimmed with lace, embroidery or a pleated frill. It could also be made in tiers and tucked into the waist belt. Popular from 1820 until 1835.

Necklines
Page 178

Basic/Plain/Jewel: A simple round neckline which would be faced.

U-Neckline: A deep neckline in the shape of a 'U'.

Scoop: A shallow but wide neckline.

Square: A square neckline which would be faced with mitred corners.

Horseshoe: A deep horseshoe-shaped neckline which would be faced.

Built-Up/Funnel: A high neckline that extends up the neck.

Sweetheart: A feminine, angular, shaped neckline that frames the breasts and neck.

Décolleté: A deep and wide neckline popular in the nineteenth century.

Wide Square: As the name suggests a wide, square-shaped neckline that would be faced.

V-Neckline: A faced V-shaped neckline.

Halter: The bodice of a garment is extended round the neck to form straps and a fastening. There is usually only a band of fabric across the back.

Bateau: A wide and shallow neckline that would be faced.

Slashed: A shallow but wide neckline, it is effectively a slit in the garment that is faced.

Sabrina: A wide but shallow neckline that has insets over the shoulder. These may be in a contrast or self-fabric.

One Shoulder: An asymmetrical neckline where the garment is supported by strapping on one shoulder only. The other is bared.

Keyhole: A jewel neckline with a slit at the front or the back which is faced and fastened, edge to edge, at the neck with a single button and rouleau loop.

Scalloped: A decoratively edged neckline that would be faced.

Inset: A jewel neckline with a slit that has an elasticated insertion.

Racing/Athletic: The main focus is on the back where the neckline and armholes are cut away to create an 'X' effect. Used in sportswear and casual wear.

Envelope: A wide neckline where the back overlaps over the front and is usually made from a knitted fabric and trimmed with a fine rib.

Crew: A snug-fitting neckline trimmed with a knitted rib as in tee shirts and sweatshirts.

Wrap-over Bateau: Similar to the envelope neckline but with a narrower overlap not quite reaching to the sleeve. This example is finished with a knitted rib.

Strapless (Princess Line): A princess line bodice with a band and a notched front but no straps for support.

Off the Shoulder: A feminine neckline where the shoulders are bared revealing the whole neck.

High Cowl: A draped neckline, usually cut on the bias to create more soft folds of draping. This example has a high cowl draping from a funnel or built up type neckline.

Mitred Neck: A square shaped neckline finished with a deep band with mitred corners.

Cowl Inset: See **high cowl**. There is a large inset of fabric, cut on the cross, to allow for soft drapes.

Elasticised: A full neckline that is controlled by elastication.

Drawstring: As the elasticised neckline but here controlled with an adjustable drawstring.

Wide Cowl: See the **high cowl** but here wider and very draped.

Graduated Ruffle: A V-shaped inset of fabric that is trimmed with a pleated and graduated ruffle. The graduation ends at the point of the 'V'.

Sugar Bag: A full neckline that is pulled together with a drawstring or band a few inches down from the edge, this creates a frill effect.

Ruffle Set-in Seam: A curved neckline with an inset of fabric outlined with a pleated ruffle.

Pleated Ruffle: A V-shaped neckline trimmed by a graduated and pleated frill.

Circular Ruffle: Rather like the Pierrot collar but not as deep.

Waist and Hemlines
Page 179

Empire Line: A high waistline named from the Empire period in France.

No Vent: There are no vents in this tailored jacket.

Vented Hem: Like the double vent but used on coat hems to help in movement on a straight garment.

Dropped Waist: The opposite to the high waist, here the line is dropped to almost the hip. There is no limit to how far the line can drop.

Single Vent: The centre back seam is open at the bottom. The vent is faced and the other side is wrapped under to create a smart finish.

Basic Curved Shirt: A shirt hemline, longer in the back than the front.

High Waist: Like the empire line, but here the line is on a separate garment, a skirt.

Bandless and Faced: There is no waistband so the waist edge of the garment is finished with a facing.

Double Vent: Partly open seams on both sides of a tailored jacket.

Poncho Trimmed: Decorative trimming on a V-shaped hemline.

Waistband: A strip of fabric folded and used to finish a skirt or trouser waistline.

Hipster: A low-slung waistline with a band that follows the shape of the body.

Peplum: A short, flared shirt that is laid over another garment, here a straight skirt. A peplum may also be attached to a jacket, see **peplum jacket**.

V-Notched and Faced: A V-shape is cut into the hemline and is faced to finish it.

Wrap Over: One side is wrapped over another and button fastened into place.

Paper Bag: A full waist that is controlled by a belt or strap allowing a frill effect to form.

Dropped Back: The back hem is longer than the front – used in dresses, shirts, coats, jackets etc.

Yoke: The garment is split into two. Here the yoke is a flat piece of fabric from which pleats are suspended.

Shaped Waist: There is no waistband and the waistline is shaped and faced.

Drawstring: The fullness at the waist is drawn up with a drawstring in a casing.

Shaped Waistband: The waistband is shaped. The band would have to be constructed of two separate pieces rather than a folded straight band.

Nightshirt: A curved hem, the back being longer than the front as in traditional nightshirts.

BIBLIOGRAPHY

A Dictionary of English Costume 900–1900. C.W. and P.E. Cunnington and Charles Beard. Adam and Charles Black, London 1976.

A Fashion Alphabet. Janey Ironside. Haro, London 1968.

A Guide to Casual Clothes: Fundamentals of Men's Fashion Design (2nd edn). Edmund B. Roberts and Gary Onishenko. Fairchild, New York 1985.

A History of Fashion: A Visual Survey of Costume from Ancient Times. Douglas Gorsline. Fitzhouse, London 1991.

A History of Shoe Fashions. Eunice Wilson. Pitman, London 1969.

Arms and Uniforms, 18th Century to the Present Day. Liliane and Fred Funcken. Ward Lock, London 1972.

Borse e Valigie (Bags and Suitcases). Litizia Bordignon Elestic. Itinerari D'immagnini, Milan 1989.

Children's Clothes Since 1750. Clare Rose. Batsford, London 1989.

Children's Costume in America 1607–1910. Estelle Ansley Worrell. Charles Scribner, New York 1980.

Concerning Clogs. Bob Dobson. Dalesman Books, Clapham 1979.

Contemporary Japanese Design. Sian Evans, Collins & Brown, 1991, London.

Corsets and Crinolines. Norah Waugh. Batsford, London 1954.

Costume 1066–1966. John Peacock. Thames and Hudson, London 1990.

Costume Patterns and Designs. Max Tilke. Magna Books, Wigston, Leicester 1990.

Costume Through the Ages. Introduced by James Laver. A Touchstone Book. Simon and Schuster, New York 1961.

Decades of Beauty: The Changing Image Of Women 1890s to 1990s. Kate Mulvey and Melissa Richards, Hamlyn, London, 1998.

Design and Communication. Tony Lawler. Longman, Harlow 1989.

Design and Designing. Ian Burden, John Morrison and John Twyford. Longman, London 1988.

Designing Apparel Through the Flat Pattern (4th edn). Ernestine Kopp, Vittorina Rolfe and Beatrice Zelin. Fairchild Publications, New York 1973.

Dress in Detail: From Around the World. Rosemary Crill, Jennifer Wearden and Verity Wilson, V & A Publications, London 2002.

Dressing and Undressing for the Seas. Irina Lindsay. Ian Henry Publications, Hornchurch 1983.

English Children's Costume Since 1775. Drawn by Iris Brooke, introduction by James Laver. Adam and Charles Black, London 1930.

Fairchild's Designer's/Stylist's Handbook, Part One. Debbie Ann Gioello. Fairchild Publications, New York 1980.

Fashion Accessories Since 1500. Geoffrey Warren. Unwin Hyman, London 1987.

Fashion Production Terms (Language of Fashion Series). Debbie Ann Gioello and Beverly Berke. Fairchild, New York 1979.

Four Hundred Years of Fashion. Natalie Rothstein (ed.). Victoria and Albert Museum in Association with William Collins, London 1984.

Good Garb – A Practical Guide to Practical Clothing. William Dasheff and Laura Dearborn. A Delta Book, Dell Publishing, New York 1980.

Guide to Fashion Merchandise, Knowledge. Ruth Tolman. Milady Publishing, The Bronx, New York 1973.

Handbook of English Costume in the 20th Century, 1900–1950. Alan Mansfield and Phillis Cunnington. Faber and Faber, London 1973.

History of Children's Costume. Elizabeth Ewing. Batsford, London 1986.

How to Draw Children. Priscilla Pointer. The Studio, London 1946.

In Vogue – Six Decades of Fashion (3rd edn). Georgina Howell. Penguin Books, London 1979.

Lingerie: A Lexicon of Style. Caroline Cox, Scriptum Editions, London, 2000.

Millers Collecting Fashion & Accessories. Carol Harris, Octopus Publishing, London 2000.

One World of Fashion. M.D.C. Crawford. Fairchild Publications, New York 1946.

Punk. Stephen Colegrave and Chris Sullivan, Cassell, London 2004.

Shoes: A Lexicon of Style. Valerie Steele, Scriptum Editions, London, 1998.

The Complete Handbook of Athletic Footwear. Melvyn P. Cheskin with Kel J. Sherkin and Barry T. Bates. Fairchild Publications, New York 1987.

The Dictionary of Costume. R Turner Wilcox. Batsford, London 1970.

The Technique of Fashion Design. Brenda Naylor. Batsford, London 1975.

The Timeline of World Costume. Claudia Muller. Thames and Hudson, London 1993.

The Twentieth Century. Penelope Bryde. Batsford, London 1993.

The X-Ray Picture Book of Your Body. David Salariya and Kathryn Senior. Parallel Books, Bristol 1995.

Visual Design in Dress. Marian L. Davis. Prentice-Hall, Englewood Cliffs, New Jersey 1980.

INDEX